TILL DEATH DO US PART

Passion within Fault

Brandon Gentry

1

"Clarence, come on, man, the game starts in about twenty minutes; we need to get down to the bar before it gets packed."

Clarence walked out of the bathroom to see his roommate, Jason, wearing his favorite jacket.

"First off, before we leave, I need for you to take that jacket off." he started to walk towards Jason.

"Aww, man, why can't I wear it?" Jason stood still with a huge grin on his face.

"I told you a million times, J, my dad gave me that jacket, and nobody wears it but me."

Clarence held out his hand and waited for Jason to take off his big blue jacket which had his dad's initials written on the sleeve.

"Aww shit, man, I forgot. I'm sorry, man." He took the jacket off and handed it to Clarence.

Clarence's dad gave him the jacket just a week before he passed away from cancer. "And besides, it don't even fit you the same way it fits me," he said with a big smile on his face. Jason was twice the size of Clarence. Not too big and far from small. Broad shoulders, and he stood about 6'4, but he weighed about 260lbs. Clarence wasn't too far behind in height. He was about 6'2, but he weighed about 175lbs.

"Man, I make everything I wear look good, now come on, man, before the bar gets packed." They began to walk out of their apartment.

It was a cold Saturday night. Pretty much a typical Saturday night for the two roommates. They'd go down to the local bar, throw down a few beers, and catch the big football games. "Man, I hope it's some fresh meat down at the bar, I need to get laid." Jason usually referred to a new group of women as fresh meat. "Man, why you always talking about getting laid? You know you're still a virgin."

Clarence looked at Jason and began to laugh.

"Now, come on, bro, you've been my roommate all through college and two years after; you know you've heard the banging on my walls many nights."

They made their way into the bar.

"Man, all these years I think I've seen you bring one girl home, and she wasn't very easy on the eyes."

Clarence waved at the waiter and held up two fingers signaling for him to bring them two beers.

"If you're talking about Bianca, I told you she like having a mustache, and I actually thought it made her look sexy. It brings out her eyes"

Clarence burst out laughing as the crowd of people turned to look and see.

"Man, you never seem to amaze me, but DAMN look at the group of girls who just walked in!"

Jason turned his neck so quick it was surprising he didn't wind up with whiplash.

"That's what I'm talking about right there, all of them are my type. Which one do you want?"

A group of about five women walked into the bar.

"Alright, J, look, let me do the talking because you always seem to mess things up when we get around a fine group of women."

They both stood up and began to walk into the group's direction. "Man, all that matters to me, Clarence, is that I get laid tonight." Clarence seemed to have his eyes set on one of the women from the minute she walked into the bar.

"Hey, how are you doing?" He held out his hand to shake the woman's hand. "My name is Clarence, I've never seen you in here before."

The woman had a smile on her face, and she met his hand with a handshake.

"My name is Ashley, this is my first time here. Me and my girls decided to try something new".

There was a long stare down between the two of them. Neither one of them looked away the whole time the other would speak. There was that whole "love at first sight" kind of feeling. "Well, Ashley, it's nice to meet you, this here is my friend, J—" Before Clarence could even finish introducing Jason, he cut him off.

"My name is Jason, but everybody calls me Big J"

He looked down to his private area then looked back up to the group of beautiful women.

"And I'm guessing they call you that because of the size of your head right?"

One of the women stood up to shake Jason's hand. He stuck his hand out to shake hers, and they both had the same stare down as

Clarence and Ashley, only theirs was more of a lust at first sight instead of love.

"This is my friend, Brittany"

She pointed to the woman who had given Jason a handshake. The other three girls had gotten up because they were just a tad bit offended from the sexual gesture Jason had made. "Do you guys want to sit and have a beer or two with us?"

Ashley wasn't your normal shy woman or the type to play hard to get. She happened to be very aggressive. She stood at about 5'7. Big brown eyes and long black hair

"Yeah, sure, we would love to," Jason spoke very loud and clear while still staring at Brittany. They all sat down, and Clarence again signaled the waiter to bring drinks only this time he held up four fingers instead of two.

"So, what do you ladies do for a living" Clarence asked with a gentle tone. It was his way of trying to sound like less of a player and more of a gentleman.

"Well, I actually work at a clinic, I'm an assistant"

The waiter came by and gave everyone a beer.

"Oh ok that's cool, I like that"

"And what about you, miss Brittany?"

Brittany still had her eyes on Jason and didn't even bother to look over towards Clarence.

"I'm whatever you want me to be, BIG J"

Which brought a smile to Jason's face. Brittany was just as aggressive as Ashley, only she was more promiscuous. She had hazel eyes and short black hair. She's the woman who happens to be in the hair salon every weekend, so the short hair was temporary.

"So, Big J, you wanna go outside and talk a little?" Before she could even finish her question, Jason was already to his feet.

"Clarence, we're going to go outside and uhh, get to know each other a little better." All Ashley could do was laugh and shake her head. It wasn't the first time she saw her best friend leave with a guy to try and "get to know him a little better". They both hurried out of the bar.

2

"So, Clarence, tell me, do you have a girlfriend?"

She asked her question then began to take a sip from her beer.

"Not at the moment I don't, but in due time, I will."

She leaned her head back, and her smile turned into a frown.

"In due time, what exactly does that mean?"

Clarence chuckled a little.

"It means if things turn out the way I hope they do, then a woman I just met will be mine, after I get to know her of course."

Ashley wasn't really the type to beat around the bush. She happened to be more straight forward, only she was very attracted to Clarence, so she figured she'd play along.

"Is that right, well maybe that woman has the same idea, but I don't think she has time to play games, so you might want to make sure you approach her the way a man should."

Now, the conversation quickly became serious.

"Of course I will, if I'm anything, I'm a man first."

The two were completely ignoring the football game as the crowded bar began to rumble with loud cheers.

"But hey, how bout we finish off these beers and back to my place to talk; it's more quiet there."

It may have sounded like a good idea to Ashley, only she wasn't as fast as her friend Brittany.

"I wish I could, but I have to get up early for work in the morning, maybe we can catch up another time."

She finished off her beer and stood to her feet. Clarence stood up so fast he almost knocked his beer over.

"Ok, that's understandable, we just so happen to meet accidently this time, I don't want the next time to be the same, you know."

They both stared at each other yet again.

"Clarence, do you want my phone number?" She stood with her hands on her hips.

"Yeah, that would be nice."

He pulled his cell phone out of his pocket and powered it on.

"You don't have to beat around the bush with me, sweetheart, just speak your mind."

She grabbed his phone and put her number in it.

"Now, please don't be the type to bug me, I can't stand that"

She had a serious tone but also a smile on her face. Clarence made his way back to the apartment. As soon as he stuck his key in the door Jason opened it and Brittany quickly made her way out.

"Nice meeting you, Clarence."

She shouted as she made her way down the stairs.

"Same to you," He shouted back, but she didn't even turn back.

"Man, what did you do to her, J?"

Clarence took off his jacket and threw it on the sofa.

"Oh, I didn't do anything out of the ordinary; we were just getting to know each other a little better."

He stood there with a big grin on his face.

"So, anyway what happened between you and Ashley? Did she turn you down? Because you sure did come home alone."

Jason made his way into the kitchen and reached into the ice box to pull out two beers.

"Turned down? Come on, man, you've known me long enough to know that I don't get turned down."

Clarence snatched a beer out of Jason's hand and made his way to sit on the sofa.

"Well then, where is she, you should have brought her home and get into her pants like I did."

He sat next to Clarence and slammed his feet onto the coffee table.

"She said she had to work early in the morning—damn, you seem to be more worried about her than me."

They looked at each other, and then burst into laughter.

"Whatever, man, I was just asking, but I gotta go to bed gotta get up early in the morning."

Jason jumped up and went into his room and closed the door. The next morning, Clarence made his way to work with Ashley on his mind. The day at work went by pretty quick with not too much to do. So, Clarence didn't waste any time getting home once his shift was over. He made his way to the apt and pulled out his cell phone as soon as he walked through the door. He called Ashley, and she picked up after the third ring.

"Hello," she said

"Hey, Ashley, what's up this is Clarence from the other night."

He was breathing so hard. It could have been the fact that he ran up the stairs, or he was nervous.

"Oh hey, Clarence, I'm just now getting off work; how was your day?"

There was a slight pause between the two.

"My day was ok, Ashley, and to be honest, I've been wanting to talk to you all day. I hope that doesn't sound weird."

Ashley chuckled. She was actually blushing. Of course, Clarence had no idea.

"Well, I wanted to invite you over tonight to my place, so I can make you dinner."

Her smile was so big, it was almost like Clarence could see it through the phone.

"I would love to, but wait, can you cook? I mean, I work at the clinic, but I don't want to be a patient there."

They both laughed.

"Oh trust me, you won't. I'm pretty good in the kitchen. All you have to do is bring that pretty smile that you're wearing right now."

She looked around to see if there was somebody watching her.

"How did…"

She stopped in the middle of her question, and it made her smile even more.

"Ok, I'll be there around eight, is that ok?"

"That's perfect. I'll see you tonight."

They both hung up the phone, smiling from ear to ear. Eight o'clock made its way around very quickly. Ashley made it at about eight-o-five. The food was still cooking but just about ready. There was a knock on the door, and Clarence went to open it. He thought about taking off the apron he had on but chose not to. He opened the door to see Ashley wearing a tight fitting yellow dress. She thought about wearing black but didn't want to seem like she was being boring and too safe, so she wore the yellow to bring out her personality. When the door opened, the aroma from the kitchen struck her in the nose as she made her way into the apartment.

"Wow that smells nice. What is it?"

Clarence led her to the dinner table.

"Just wait, you'll see."

He pulled out her chair, and she took a seat.

"Just give me a second, and dinner will be served."

"Ashley, do you drink wine?"

She turned and faced the kitchen from her seat.

"I sure do."

She turned back, and then Clarence made his way to the table with two glasses filled with Merlot.

"I'll be right back with the dinner."

He was moving quickly like a waiter. He made his way back to the table with two plates that had blackened tilapia and vegetables.

"You mean to tell me you cooked this all by yourself?"

Ashley had a big smile on her face. She wasn't used to a man actually cooking for her.

"Yes, why is that a surprise to you?"

He placed the plates on the table and sat down.

"I'm just not used to having a man cook for me. It smells good, but I'll be the judge on whether it tastes good."

They both laughed. Clarence held out his hands.

"Let's say our grace, so you can get to judging"

She placed her hands in his, and they said a prayer over the meal.

"So, Ashley, tell me what's a pretty woman like you doing single?"

She held up her finger to let him know that she would need a minute to respond because she had already began to eat.

"Well, I've always had issues with men, I'm a little picky, and at the same time, I have a hard time trusting men."

She spoke in a serious tone while looking Clarence in the eye.

"And why is that, I mean, I know us males can be difficult to deal with, but we're not all that bad." He tried to throw a little humor her way.

"I was raped when I was seventeen."

3

Clarence's smile turned into a frown. Clarence didn't know how to respond to her confession. He felt a little awkward because that was something he didn't expect to hear on the first night.

"Damn, Ashley, that's terrible. I'm sorry, I wouldn't have asked that question if I would have known." He looked her into her eyes the whole time to assure her that he was being sincere.

"It's ok, you had no idea. You were just breaking the ice, and that's understandable."

This seemed to be a conversation she was used to because she confessed with so much ease, and she seemed to be very comfortable. Either that or she wasn't much of a drinker, and the wine hit her quick.

"The crazy thing is, Clarence, it wasn't by a boyfriend or a stranger on the streets, it was my step-father."

This made Clarence put down his fork.

"Are you serious?"

There weren't too many words coming from Clarence because he had no idea what to say.

"I'm sorry, Clarence, I'm telling you a sad story, and I'm just messing up our nice little dinner. I'm so embarrassed."

She placed the palm of her hand on her forehead to try and hide her eyes.

"It's ok, Ashley, I understand you were just venting a little. Don't worry, I'm not here to judge you"

That made her move her hand and look up with a smile.

12

"I hope I haven't scared you off already; that usually takes me three dates to do."

They both laughed loud, and the comfort was restored. After they finished dinner, Clarence took the dishes and placed them into the sink.

"Do you want help with the dishes?"

Ashley asked as she stood up.

"Not at all, you don't have to worry about lifting a finger tonight."

She smiled.

"Well, as much as I don't want to, I have to get going because I have to be to work early in the morning."

This came as a surprise to Clarence because he didn't expect her to leave so early.

"Are you sure you don't want to stay just a little longer?"

"I would love to, but I can't, maybe next time."

Clarence made sure he didn't show the disappointment in his face, so he kept a smile.

"Speaking of next time, when will that be?"

He grabbed her coat from the couch and got behind her and helped her put it on.

"I want it to be as soon as possible, Clarence, I enjoyed you tonight, and I also enjoyed your cooking."

She turned to face him.

"Well how about next Saturday we go catch a movie or something"

"That sounds great just as long as you let me pick the movie"

Again they both shared a laugh.

"Of course anything you want to see is fine with me"

She gave him a hug and just as soon as he began to pull away, she snuck in a kiss.

"Wow!"

Clarence leaned back and smiled at Ashley.

"I'm sorry, Clarence, I don't know what I was thinking. I guess I got caught in the moment. I gotta go."

She turned and hurried out the door.

"No, wait!"

Clarence tried to stop her, but she had already made her way out of the apartment. He turned and went to sit on the sofa. All he could do was wonder why she would kiss him then run away so quickly. He then heard a knock on the door. That's when he jumped, up hoping it was Ashley. To his surprise, it was Jason.

"Man, you looking like you're happy to see me. Give daddy a kiss."

He laughed and gave Clarence a little push to get through the door.

"Quit playing around."

Clarence said as he closed the door.

"Man, what you doing knocking on the door anyway?"

They both went towards the kitchen.

"I forgot my key when me and Brittany went running out of here."

Jason went towards the fridge and pulled out some beer. This happened to be an everyday thing for these two. Whenever they would both be in the house at the same time, they just had to share a beer or two and talk about the day they had.

"So, what happened between you and Ashley; did you get lucky?"

Jason went and plopped down on the couch like he had a long day at work.

"To be honest, no, I didn't. All I got was a peck on the lips."

Jason took a sip from his beer and looked towards Clarence.

"A peck? Man, you wined and dined this woman, and all you settled for was a peck? You're better than me."

They both laughed.

"Yeah, man, the night was so awkward, I'm confused as hell."

"What you confused about? You just don't have the charm anymore, or maybe you never had it."

Again, they both laughed.

"Naw, man, it's crazy. We were having a good time, and then she just tells me how she was raped as a little girl. I didn't know what to say to that."

Jason's jaw dropped.

"What kind of person tells that kind of a story on the first date?"

He puts his beer on the table

"She sounds crazy, man, you have to leave her alone. Don't get caught up messing with a girl like that."

Clarence took another sip from his drink and placed it on the table.

"J, it's not like she told me she murdered somebody. I wanna get to know this girl. There's something different about her, and I'm willing to find out."

Jason shook his head in disbelief.

"Well, you can get to know her then, but don't say I didn't warn you. She sounds crazy."

"Whatever, man. So, what's going on with you and Brittany?"

Jason stood to his feet.

"Well, unlike you, my man, I got to know her friend very well, and we are going to be seeing a lot more of each other. Don't be jealous, just be happy you know me."

4

The next morning came pretty fast. When Clarence woke up, he got himself dressed and headed to work. While on his way to work, he pulled out his phone and sent a text message to Ashley.

"I really enjoyed your company last night. You looked beautiful, but why did you run out so quick? Give me a call when you get a chance."

The day went by, and he received no text or call back from Ashley. This would continue for the whole week. He texted and called a couple times but got no response. Finally, on a rainy Sunday night, his phone rang, and it was Ashley.

"Ashley, what's going on? I've been trying to contact you. Was my cooking that bad you just ran out without saying anything?"

"Clarence, your food was amazing, and I really do like you. I just felt so embarrassed about the whole night."

"What was there to be so embarrassed about? You didn't do anything wrong."

"Well, first it was the story I told you, then I just kissed you out of the blue. I felt like a mess."

Clarence snickered a little.

"It's ok, sweetheart, I didn't mind. I just thought maybe you didn't like me."

"Oh no, I do like you there's just something going on with me that I want to tell you, but I just don't know how."

Clarence let out a deep sigh.

"Well, just speak your mind."

"Well, Clarence, you see, I'm going to have to talk to you in person about this."

"Well, where are you, Ashley? Can you meet me somewhere?"

There was a long silence.

"Hello? Ashley, are you there?"

"Yes, I'm still here, but I have to go, Clarence. I'll have to call you later."

She hung up the phone before he could even respond. Clarence said hello a few times until he heard nothing but the dial tone. The night ended, and he received no call back from her. As the morning came, Clarence woke up to someone knocking at the door. He jumped out of bed and hurried towards the door.

"HOLD ON! DAMN!"

He opened the door and to his surprise it was Ashley.

"Hey, Clarence, I'm sorry to come by so early without calling but—"

Clarence kissed her before she could even finish her sentence.

"I'm sorry, Ashley, I owed you one."

They both laughed.

"Tell me what's going on. Why do you keep avoiding me?"

He led her to the couch, and they both sat down. Ashley took a deep breath before she began to speak.

"Ok, Clarence, I don't want to upset you, but I feel it's best I tell you before things get too serious," She looked him directly in his eyes as she spoke.

"My ex-boyfriend has moved back. We talked, and now we're engaged."

Clarence shook his head repeatedly.

"I'm so sorry, Clarence, I should've told you. I hope you're not upset, I would really like for us to be friends."

Clarence looked at Ashley and smiled.

"I think it's best that you leave."

He stood up and walked towards the door. He then opened it and waited for her to leave. Ashley stood up and walked towards the door. She apologized again. As she got closer to the door, she reached in to give Clarence a hug, but he pulled back.

"Please, just leave, Ashley."

She walked out, and he closed the door. They both leaned against the door as if they were leaning against each other. Jason woke up and walked out of his room and saw Clarence leaned against the wall.

"Clarence what the hell you doing, are you drunk?'

He began to laugh until he saw the seriousness in his friends face.

"Umm, what's going on?"

"Ashley just left."

Clarence stood up and walked to the couch to sit down. Jason followed behind him.

"Well, damn, she must've really put it on you. She had you looking like you could barely stand up straight."

Again, he tried to make light of the situation, but Clarence didn't budge.

"Man, that's the least of my worries right now, she just told me she's engaged!"

Jason leaned back as Clarence shared the bad news.

"See, I told you that bitch was crazy, but you didn't believe me."

"Jason, don't be disrespectful, man. Act like you have a mother."

They both looked at each other straight face and all.

"What the hell does my mother have to do with this?"

"I really can't believe you're that much of an ass, Jason."

Clarence stood to his feet and walked towards the kitchen.

"See, that's why she didn't give you any, she came over here, drunk your wine, and went home and put it on her fiancé," He laughed loud this time without stopping.

"That's bullshit, Jason, I don't believe she's telling the truth."

"Man, why the hell would someone lie about being engaged? That's stupid." He then walked into the kitchen.

"I know it sounds crazy, but the way she's been acting, the way she told me—it just doesn't seem believable. It's something going on with her, but it's not an engagement that's making her act that way." Clarence began to walk towards his room then his phone vibrated. As he reached into his pocket to pull it out Jason kept talking.

"Ok, you keep trying to figure this girl out, and you're going to get your feelings hurt. Just give it up; she's one lying broad. I told you that." Clarence paid him no attention and walked straight into his room and closed the door. He began reading a text message that was from Ashley. It read:

"Clarence, I'm sorry for leading you on. You seem like such a great guy, but I just felt like I didn't deserve a guy like you, and I wouldn't want to hurt you. So, I just felt it was best for me to pull back before things even got serious. It just so happens that my ex came back into the picture."

Clarence put his phone down before he even finished reading the message. He didn't believe a word she was telling him. He knew in the back of his mind that it was something deeper than what she was telling him. He figured he'd make it his business to find out.

5

The next morning, Clarence woke up to the sounds of laughter in the living room. He pushed himself out of the bed and walked out to see Jason and Brittany sitting on the couch.

"Hey, Clarence, did we wake you?" Brittany yelled out as she turned to look Clarence's way.

"Oh naw, I usually wake up this early to go jogging on my off days." He walked behind the two of them and gave a slight nudge to Jason and made his way to the kitchen.

"Oh ok, that's cool." Brittany stood to her feet and followed him into the kitchen.

"So, how are you and Ashley doing? Are you guys getting serious, thinking about marriage, maybe two or three kids? Tell me details, sir, so I can start planning the wedding; plus, I need to slim down, so I can fit into a nice dress. I don't want to be a maid of honor looking like a whale." Clarence looked at her with a very confused look.

"First off, you talk too damn fast. Second, I thought Ashley just got engaged to her ex-boyfriend?" Brittany let out a huge gasp.

"Are you serious? Is that what she told you? I hope you're not talking about Robert the guy who constantly cheated on her and always made her feel like crap. Not the same Robert who would leave her without her car just so he could creep through the night. Not the same Robert who made my friend so depressed and always had me running to her side every time I thought she would overdose on ice cream and cake. You know how us women like to eat when we're sad."

Again, this brought a confused look to Clarence's face.

"Damn, can you take a breath? You just said all of that, and nothing is making sense to me right now. Yesterday, she told me that she had to end things between us before they got serious because she felt like she didn't deserve me, and he came back in town, so she figured it was best for her to go back to what she was used to."

"Really, Clarence, is that what she told you? I need to talk to my friend because she better not be getting married to that asshole and didn't tell me." She pulled out her phone and called Ashley's phone, but it went straight to voicemail.

"I really don't remember word for word what she told me. I mean, she lost me when she said that she didn't deserve me, but I felt like she wasn't telling me the truth. I could tell by her tone that she wasn't being honest, but why would she lie?" Brittany grabbed her purse and her keys and then she turned back to Clarence.

"I don't know what's going on, but I've never known her to be a liar. Now, I do know there's something going on with her that may be the reason why she pulled back, but she's going to have to tell you that herself. I'm going to go to her house and talk to her."

She headed towards the door, but first, she leaned over the couch to give Jason a kiss. He seemed uninterested in the conversation the two of them were having, his face was glued to the television as he watched highlights from the night before.

"Wait, Brittany, why can't you tell me? You see she can't seem to tell me what's really going on, so please just let me know." Brittany opened the door and turned to speak before she walked completely out.

23

"She's a special girl, Clarence, I really mean that, but this issue she needs to tell you herself. I feel it's best that way. Trust me, in due time, I'm sure she will. Just give her some time."

With that said she walked outside and closed the door behind her. Things became even more confusing for Clarence than from the night before. Brittany left their apartment and made her way to Ashley's. She got out of her car and went straight to the door. She kept knocking until Ashley opened.

"Why didn't you tell me you were getting married, and who are you getting married to?" She yelled out as she pushed her way into Ashley's apartment. "Brittany, calm down, damn!" Ashley walked into the living room. Brittany walked right behind her.

"So, I'm supposed to be your best friend, and you didn't even tell me? I need to know what's going on."

"Brittany, I'm not getting married, there's not going to be a wedding in my future unless I'm going to someone else's." Brittany just stared at her friend.

"So, why did you tell Clarence that you were getting married? Why would you lie to him like that? He seems like a good guy. I mean, I know you guys are just getting to know each other and all, but that's not the way you start things off." She continued to stare down her friend as she waited for a response.

"That's just the thing, he does seem like a good guy, and like you said, we were just getting started, but I had to pull back." She slumped into the couch.

"Ashley, you're not making any sense please help me understand." She moved from the love seat to the couch to sit closer to her friend.

"I don't deserve a guy like him. I mean, he cooked for me, he pulled out my chair, he looked me in my eyes when I was talking, he gave me wine, and even though I got a little tipsy he didn't even try to make a move on me. He seemed like the perfect gentleman, and I know that's how all men start out, but he just give's off a different vibe." She sat up on the couch.

"I'm not proud of some of the things I've done in my past; that's why I feel like I don't deserve him, but I mean, I'm a good woman. I'm just tired of being hurt."

"Ashley, we've all made mistakes in our past, but if we continue to let that be the reason for not allowing good people in our lives, then we're going to be miserable old women. If you feel like he's a good guy, don't be afraid to open up to him. You can take things slow, but don't push him away. I mean, who knows, he could be Mr. Right." A few tears began to fall from Ashley's face.

"I've done things in my past I'm not proud of, but you see I've been able to open up to Jason." "Brittany, the only thing you're opening up are your legs." They both began to laugh. Then Ashley's phone rang. It was from a familiar number, so she answered it. She tried to lower the volume so Brittany couldn't hear, but he spoke before she had a chance. "I'm down the street from your house. We need to talk." Before she had a chance to tell him that it wasn't a good time, there was a knock at the

25

door. Brittany just so happened to be closer to the door, so she went to open it up.

6

As she opened the door the man standing on the outside jaw dropped completely. Brittany yelled to him

"WHAT THE HELL ARE YOU DOING HERE?!" Jason just stood there quiet as if he was trying to get his story together.

"Before you assume the wrong thing, let me explain." Brittany slammed the door in his face and turned her attention back to Ashley.

"Ashley, what is Jason doing at your front door?" Ashley stood up but before she could speak Brittany yelled out again.

"How does he even know where you live?" Jason knocked at the door again. Brittany turned and opened the door again.

"Brittany let me in so we can all sit down and talk" She opened the door and allowed him to step inside. He walked in with an awkward look on his face. Ashley stood rubbing her hands looking very nervous.

"Somebody needs to explain what the hell is going on here."

"Brittany, calm down and let's sit down and talk." Jason reached to place his hand on her shoulder, and she pulled back quickly.

"Don't touch me, and I'm not going to sit down." He pulled his hands back.

"Ok, first, let me explain how me and Ashley know each other." Brittany turned to face Ashley. It seemed as if she wasn't paying attention to what Jason was saying, but she just didn't care to look at him while he was speaking.

"Me and Ashley met a while back. We went on a couple dates and that's it, nothing happened between the two of us." Brittany turned back to face Jason.

"We never hugged, we never kissed, nothing at all. Just dinner and conversation—that's it." "So, why didn't you two tell me?" She walked to the couch and sat down with a disgusted look on her face. Ashley came to sit next to her, and Jason remained standing.

"Brittany, I promise I was going to tell you, I just didn't know how."

"What do you mean you didn't know how?" Before Ashley could respond Brittany cut her off.

"All you had to do was say 'Hey, I know that guy, we went out and had dinner a few times', then I would have never spoke to him." "

I'm sorry, Brittany, I really am, but like he said, it was a long time ago and nothing happened. I just thought it wasn't that big of a deal, but don't be mad at him because I told him that I'd tell you myself." Jason sat down on the love seat.

"So, if it's not that big of a deal why didn't you say anything when we first met? It seems to me that it's more to it than what ya'll are telling me because it took some time before you two decided to tell me."

"IT'S NOT EVEN LIKE THAT BRITTANY!" Jason yelled out.

"What would've happened if I wasn't here, Jason? What were you coming over here for? I mean, if yall were gonna tell me, then why didn't you call me first and tell me to meet you over here?" She stood up and grabbed her purse and keys. Jason stood up to block her from leaving.

28

"Look, I know you're upset, I don't blame you, but don't just leave like this. I don't want you to be mad at her; be mad at me. I should've been man enough to tell you the truth." She pushed him out of the way and made her way to the door. Before she opened the door, she turned to them both.

"Ashley, is this the reason you told Clarence you were getting married? When do you plan on telling him? Jason, how could you keep this from your best friend, and you know he really likes her?" Before either one of them could answer, she opened the door and left. Jason turned and looked at Ashley.

"I'm going to go, I'm sorry, Ashley." He then walked out of the apartment. Then, her phone rang. It was Clarence, so she picked up.

"Hey, Ashley, are you busy? I was hoping we could talk."

"Yes, Clarence, we can talk. I need to tell you some things anyway. I'm on my way" Ashley hung up the phone, grabbed her purse, and walked out the door. About ten minutes later, there was a knock at Clarence's door. He rushed to open it, thinking it was Ashley, but to his surprise, it was Jason.

"Man, what are you doing knocking? Where's your key?"

"I left it in my room, but never mind that, you and I have to talk, bro."

"Well, can we make it quick, Ashley's on the way me and her have some things to talk about as well." Jason walked into the kitchen opened the fridge and grabbed two beer's. He turned to Clarence and tossed him one.

29

"Speaking of Ashley, that's kinda what I wanted to talk to you—" There was another knock at the door before Jason could finish his sentence.

"Hold your thought, bro." He turned to open the door again thinking it was Ashley but it wasn't. It was Brittany. She stood there with her hands on her hips.

"Where's Jason, me and him have to talk." Clarence opened the door, so she could see Jason standing drinking his beer. She pushed her way past Clarence and began to walk towards Jason.

"Brittany, can this wait? Me and Clarence need to talk." Brittany stopped and made her way to the sofa. She sat down, leaned back, and crossed her legs.

"Well, I'll wait right here. I mean, whatever you need to say to him, you can say in front of me. We all need to talk anyway." Jason looked at Clarence as he yelled out, "Can somebody please tell me what it is that we all have to talk—?"

Before he could finish, there was another knock at the door. Only this time, it was Ashley. Clarence opened the door, and when he saw that it was Ashley, he opened it wide, so she could see Brittany and Jason both in the living room. She hesitated to walk in until Clarence told her to come in.

"Come on in, sweetheart, we all obviously need to have a serious talk." Ashley then walked inside of the apartment.

"Ok, so, will somebody please tell me what's going on?" Nobody said a word. Everybody just looked around the room.

"Well, if nobody wants to say..."

"Jason and Ashley slept with each other!" Brittany screamed out.

Clarence dropped his beer on the floor. Then, he looked at Ashley. Her mouth dropped in surprise. He then turned his attention to Jason. Jason shook his head. Clarence then walked into his room and grabbed his car keys. He returned to the living room, picked his beer from the floor and headed towards the door. Before he opened it and walked out, he turned to look around the room full of shocked faces, and then he turned and walked out. Instead of showing his anger and slamming the door, he closed it gently and disappeared into the night.

"What the hell is your problem, Brittany? Me and Ashley never slept with each other." Ashley just stood staring at her friend whom she had known for years. She then began to speak.

"Brittany, me and Jason went out twice, that's it. I never slept with him. You know I'm not like that." Brittany stood to her feet.

"If you two never slept with each other, then why were yall keeping things a secret?" Neither of them answered. Ashley grabbed her phone and tried to call Clarence, but it went straight to voicemail.

"Thanks a lot, Brittany, now he'll probably never speak to me again."

Then, her phone vibrated. It was a text message from Clarence.

"To be honest, Ashley, I'm not even mad I'm used to being let down, so this is nothing new. I'm just glad that it happened now instead of further down the road. I wish things could've been different. You seemed like a good person—guess I was wrong." Ashley stood there staring at her phone. The whole room was quiet. Then, Jason spoke out.

31

"We have to fix this because I don't want to see my friend go down that lonely road again".

But what were they to do? At the moment, nobody had an answer. Jason and Ashley both took turn's calling Clarence's phone. Neither had any luck as they both kept getting his voicemail.

"Where do you think he went, Jason?"

"There's no telling, maybe he's just out driving around."

"Well, I have to get home. It's getting late, and I have to wake up early in the morning." She headed towards the door. Before she opened it to leave, she turned to speak to her friend.

"Brittany, I know this looks bad, and I'm sorry I didn't say anything before, but I promise you, nothing happened between me and Jason."

Brittany stood up and walk towards Ashley and gave her a hug.

"I believe you." They hugged for a while, and when they let go, Brittany went back to sit next to Jason, and Ashley walked out of the apartment. "Jason, why didn't you tell me?"

Jason let out a deep sigh.

"Better yet, why didn't you tell Clarence? You've known him almost all your life." He then raised up from his slouched position.

"I really didn't think it was that big of a deal, Brittany, I mean all we did was go out on two dates." He placed his phone on the table.

"We didn't sleep together, we didn't kiss. Hell, we didn't even hug each other, so we both felt it really wouldn't be an issue." That response brought Brittany to her feet.

"You've got to be kidding me, Jason. What do you mean not a big issue? Me and her are best friends, and you and him are like brothers. Of course, it's a big deal." Jason then stood to his feet.

"Look, Brittany, I've apologized. What else do you want me to do?" She then reached down to grab her purse and turned towards the door. She then turned around and walked to Jason, gave him a kiss, and whispered in his ear.

"Goodbye, Jason, I don't know where things will go from here between you and me, but you need to find your friend and fix things with him." She walked out of the apartment. Around one in the morning, Ashley heard a knock at her door which woke her out her sleep. She turned on almost every light in the apartment.

"Who is it?" She yelled out as she walked towards the door. There was no response, so she looked through the peep hole. It was Clarence, so she opened the door.

"What are you doing here so late, Clarence?"

"Can I come in, or are you going to talk to me like this?" She pulled the door open, so he was able to walk in.

"I was just driving around, and I felt like maybe we should talk, so I could get a better understanding on what's going on." Ashley walked towards the sofa and sat down. Clarence stood in front of the door.

"I wanted to apologize for just walking out earlier without saying a word." Ashley motioned for Clarence to come sit next to her, but he wouldn't move.

"I just can't understand why you guy's never told me anything."

"Don't you want to sit down, Clarence?" Again, he didn't move.

33

"I mean, I know things weren't that serious between us, but don't you think that's something we should have talked about? I mean, if I would've known that then I wouldn't have allowed myself to even approach you."

"But, Clarence—" He cut her off before she could even finish.

"I'm going to get my own place on the other side of town. It's time for a fresh start. Anyway, I wish you all the best."

He didn't even say goodbye. He just walked out of the apartment. Ashley just sat there, wondering why he even came over. Wondering why he asked to talk if he wasn't willing to listen to what she had to say. Wondering how she could even have such strong feelings towards a person she was still getting to know.

7

A couple of weeks went by, and nobody had heard anything from Clarence. He moved his things out of the apartment he shared with Jason. He stuck to his word and moved to the other side of town. Meanwhile, back at Ashley's house, she kept finding herself going through her phone trying her best not to call Clarence's phone. Then, there was a knock at her door. "Who is it?" she yelled out as she made her way from the kitchen. There was no response. She looked through the peep hole, and then opened the door once she realized who it was.

"What are you two doing here?" Standing at the door were Jason and Brittany.

"We just wanted to come by and make sure that you were ok. It's been a while since we've all hung out or even spoke," Brittany said as she and Jason made their way into the apartment.

"Well, I'm doing fine. I've just been working. Nothing out of the ordinary." They all made their way into the living room and sat down.

"Have you heard from Clarence at all?" Jason asked her while playing a game on his cell phone.

"Not at all, he hasn't called me or even sent a text. I haven't tried to either." Then, her phone began to ring.

"Wow, speaking of the Devil this is him right here." Brittany and Jason both turned their attention to her as she answered the phone.

"Hello, Clarence, where are you? Are you ok?" There was a long pause before he responded.

"Yes, I'm fine." Then, he let out a deep sigh.

35

"What's wrong, Clarence?" This made Brittany and Jason both sit on the edge of the couch.

"Nothing's wrong, sweetheart, just had a long day at work. I would like to see you though." That response made her let out a sigh of relief.

"Ok, Clarence when? And where?"

"Right now, Ashley, where are you?" She then stood up from her seat.

"Well, right now, I'm at home. Jason and Brittany are here as well."

Again there was a long pause.

"Ok, well, I just want to see you and nobody else. Meet me at the bar down the street from my old apartment. You know, the one we met at."

Without hesitating, she ran to her room and grabbed her purse.

"Ok, Clarence, I'm leaving my apartment now." She stopped in front of Brittany and Jason to let them know what was going on.

"I'm going to meet with Clarence." Jason stood to his feet. "Where? I have to see my boy—" Before he could finish, Ashley cut him off.

"No, he said he only wants to see me. You two stay here, I'm going to try and get him to come back, so we can all talk." Jason sat down.

"Ok, but don't take long. I don't want to be here all night. You don't even have any beer."

Ashley then walked out of the apartment. About twenty five minutes later, she arrived at the bar. She walked in to see Clarence sitting at a table by himself, so she walked up to him, and he stood from his seat and gave her a hug and a kiss on her cheek.

"Would you like a drink, Ashley?"

"No, not tonight, I'm fine, thanks for asking though." He pulled out her chair, and she sat down. Clarence made his way back to his seat.

"So, let's get straight to the point, Ashley. Never mind the how have you been questions." Ashley moved her purse from the table and placed it in a chair, so that she could see Clarence's eyes.

"Well, what is it you want to do?"

"The first night we spent together, you told me a lot of personal things that happened to you in your past; why was it so hard for you to tell me about Jason?"

"It wasn't that it was hard, Clarence, it's just, I figured since nothing happened between me and him, it wasn't a big deal." Her response brought a smirk to Clarence's face.

"Now, let's be real here, if this were me and Brittany, and we didn't tell you, wouldn't you be a little skeptical?"

"Skeptical about what, Clarence?" Before responding he took a sip from his drink.

"You know what, it doesn't even matter" He took another sip from his drink.

"Clarence, I'm going to be completely honest with you. Nothing happened between us at all. Like I said before, I'm sorry for not telling you anything. Now, either you let this situation go and we move on and start fresh, or we just move on from each other and go our separate ways because I don't have time to be going back and forth, and I'm not going to chase you down. I like you, I just don't like this situation."

They stared each other down for about a minute or so.

"Ok, you're right, maybe we should start fresh." Then, he stood to his feet and walked over to her side of the table and held out his hand.

"Come on, let's get out of here." She grab her purse then his hand. As they were walking outside, a guy who was entering the bar stopped in front of the two of them.

"Ashley, is that you? How have you been?"

Ashley stood still with a nervous look on her face. It was her ex from years ago. Ashley just waved to the guy and kept walking. The guy looked at Clarence, then shrugged his shoulders and walked into the bar. Clarence made his way outside and walked up to Ashley. Before Ashley could say anything, he spoke.

"Don't worry, sweetheart, I'm not interested in who that was. Let's just go." He put his around her waist, and they walked to the parking lot.

"So, I guess I'll call you when I make it home." Ashley pulled away from him, so that they could have a better view of each other's face.

"No, I want you to spend the night with me." Ashley looked surprised. Considering the fact that Clarence had been keeping his distance lately.

"Are you sure that's a good idea? I mean you've been drin—"

Clarence kissed her before she could even finish. He pulled her close to him and grabbed her by the butt. The longer they kissed the tighter his grip became. This seemed to turn Ashley on because she pulled back and let out a deep breath.

"Ok, come on let's go. I'll follow you".

Clarence got in his car, and Ashley got into hers. They made it to his apartment and both jumped out of their cars once they found parking spots. Ashley followed Clarence up the stairs. He lived on the third floor, so she stopped to take her heels off. Once they made it into the apartment, they began where they left off in the parking lot. Clarence picked her up, and she wrapped her legs around his waist as he carried her into the bedroom. He laid her down on the bed and climbed on top of her. He began kissing her on her neck as she let out a few moans. Neither one of them were thinking about moving too fast or anything of that nature. Ashley sat up to take off her shirt and he stopped her.

"Lay down, I don't want you to do anything. Let me handle that."

So, he ripped open her blouse and began to kiss her on her breasts. This obviously turned her on even more because her breaths became even heavier than when they first made it to the bed. Clarence unbuttoned her pants and pulled them off slowly. Then, he began to move his tongue up and down her inner thighs. He made his way to her vagina. But then he paused. He got up, and she asked,

"Clarence what's wrong?"

He placed a finger over her lips to silence her. Then, he grabbed a pillow and placed it underneath her pelvis, and she then laid back down. He made his way back down and began to breathe, so she could feel his breath on her clitoris. This built up the anticipation even more. This caused her to squirm over the bed. He then began to lick her like an ice

39

cream cone. He used deep strokes which allowed him to cover her whole vagina. His licks gradually built up intensity. She wrapped her legs around his neck which made him go even deeper.

"Oh my, God, I'm about to cum."

Her legs began to shake, and Clarence continued to lick her in the spot which made her squirm. He could feel that her body had become weak, so he pulled back and laid her legs down on the bed. He then pulled his pants off and then his shirt and climbed on top of her. As he began kissing her, she grabbed his penis and slid it inside of her vagina. Neither one of them even thought to stop and grab protection, they were both so caught up in the moment. This night would change both of their lives forever.

8

The night ended, and both Clarence and Ashley were sound asleep. Both exhausted from the passionate love making. When the morning came, and the sun made its way into Clarence's bedroom, it woke Ashley up out of her sleep. She rolled over expecting him to be right next to her, but he wasn't. This scene seemed too familiar to her. She sat up in the bed showing her frustration. Then, she grabbed her phone to call him. The ringer went off on the cell phone sitting on the night stand next to the bed.

"What the hell?"

She said as she jumped out of the bed. She then began to put on her pants. Clarence then came walking into the room holding a tray with food on it and a pair of roses.

"You're leaving already?" He asked.

"Oh no, Clarence, I was just putting my pants on" She tried to hide the frustration on her face.

"I made you breakfast; didn't really know how you liked your eggs, but I scrambled them." Ashley sat down on the bed as Clarence walked up to her with the breakfast he had prepared for her.

"Oh that's fine, I love my eggs scrambled." He then placed the tray over her lap.

"Pancakes, eggs, bacon, and grits. What are you trying to say, Clarence, that I'm fat and greedy?" Clarence laughed.

"Not at all, I just figured you'd wake up with an appetite."

They both looked each other and smiled.

41

"Well where is your food sir?"

She took a bite out of the crisp bacon.

"Whatever you don't eat, I'll eat. I didn't think to make enough for myself I just wanted to make sure I filled your stomach." This brought a look of shock to her face.

"Wait a minute, Clarence. Why are you being so nice? I thought you hated me." He then moved closer to her on the bed.

"If I hated you, then you wouldn't be with me right now, and I damn sure wouldn't have made you breakfast and last night would have not happened." That comment caused her to put down her spoon and look Clarence into his eyes.

"Clarence, about last night," She paused as they both stared each other down. "What about it?" She moved the tray from her lap onto the night stand.

"Last night, Clarence, I think you were drunk, and I was so caught up in the moment, we didn't do the right thing."

"You're right, Ashley, we didn't and I'm sorry I don't know I just couldn't help myself I felt so close to you finally" After those words there was a very long pause.

"What if I get pregnant?" She was expecting a very aggressive response from him because she leaned back after she finished.

"I was going to ask you the same exact thing, Ashley." After that she dropped her head in disgust.

"Oh my, God, I can't believe I was so stupid." She slammed her face into her hands and began to cry. This made Clarence to move closer to her and place his arm around her shoulder.

"Listen to me, Ashley, I know last night didn't go the way it should have. It happened so fast, but don't place all the blame on yourself. I mean, I wasn't much help at all. I just want you to know you're not in this situation alone. I'm just as guilty as you."

She then raised her head and looked him in his eyes.

"Clarence, but what if I'm pregnant? Of course, you're going to say 'oh I'll be here for you' and all that good stuff, but we know men say that all in the beginning. But in the end, it's always us by ourselves."

He stood up and held out his hand and nodded his head in a motion telling her to follow him. She grabbed his hand and they both walked outside to the balcony.

"I know most guys all say the same thing, and I know that last night felt good even though it was wrong. But we're both adults, we knew what we were getting ourselves into; but stop panicking so much. I mean, there's no guarantee that you're pregnant, Ashley, let's not talk about tomorrow, let's just talk about today. Let's just take it one day at a time. I know words are just words, and a lot of what men say sounds good, but I'm not the one to speak much. So, judge me by my actions, and you'll be satisfied."

Those words seemed to calm her for the moment. Clarence pulled her closer to him, and then kissed her on the lips.

"Oh my, God, I can't believe I was so stupid." She slammed her face into her hands and began to cry. This made Clarence to move closer to her and place his arm around her shoulder.

"Listen to me, Ashley, I know last night didn't go the way it should have. It happened so fast, but don't place all the blame on

43

yourself. I mean, I wasn't much help at all. I just want you to know you're not in this situation alone. I'm just as guilty as you."

She then raised her head and looked him in his eyes.

"Clarence, but what if I'm pregnant? Of course, you're going to say 'oh I'll be here for you' and all that good stuff, but we know men say that all in the beginning, but in the end, it's always us by ourselves."

He stood up and held out his hand and nodded his head in a motion, telling her to follow him. She grabbed his hand, and they both walked outside to the balcony.

"I know most guys all say the same thing, and I know that last night felt good even though it was wrong, but we're both adults. We knew what we were getting ourselves into; but stop panicking so much. I mean, there's no guarantee that you're pregnant, Ashley, let's not talk about tomorrow. let's just talk about today let's just take it one day at a time I know words are just words and a lot of what men say sound good, but I'm not the one to speak much. So, judge me by my actions, and you'll be satisfied."

Those words seemed to calm her for the moment. Clarence pulled her closer to him, and then kissed her on the lips.

"You don't have to trust me, just trust in God and everything will be ok."

After those words, he kissed her on the forehead, and they both stood and watched as the sun continued to rise.

"Clarence, can I ask you a question?"

Ashley asked as they both made their way back into the apartment.

"Sure, ask me anything." They made their way to the living room and sat on the sofa.

"Do you believe in love in first sight?" He chuckled.

"What's so funny?" She placed her legs onto his lap.

"I believe in you and me." His response brought a big smile to her face.

"That was unexpected, but I'll take it." She moved her legs from his lap and stood to her feet.

"I wish I could stay with you all day, but I have to run a few errands."

Clarence stood to his feet and grabbed her by the waist and pulled her close to him.

"So, when will I see you again, Ashley?" He kissed her lips.

"Whenever you're free, sir."

They both walked to the bedroom, so she could get her purse. Clarence wasn't ready for her to leave. He still had the night before on his mind. Ashley made her way into the restroom to wash her face. As soon as she pulled the wash cloth down from her face, she looked into the mirror and saw Clarence standing behind her completely naked. She turned to face him as he walked up to her. Now, he towered over her, standing at 6'2. Ashley was 5'7. So, when he kissed her, he always had to lean down, and she had to stand on her toes. To avoid having to do that this time, Clarence picked her up and placed her on the counter next to the sink. They began to kiss, and he pulled her pants along with her underwear down slowly.

"Wait, Clarence, I'm going to be late. I have to get my nails..."
Before she could finish, he was already inside of her. This time didn't last
as long as the night before because Ashley had to get to the other side of
town to run her errands.

9

A few weeks passed by, and Clarence and Ashley found themselves getting closer to one another. They had been on a few dates and basically had been around each other every day. If they weren't together in person, they were either texting one another or on the phone. One night, Clarence went into his normal hangout spot to grab a few beers after work.

"Hey there, young man, what you having tonight?"

The bartender called out as soon as he saw Clarence walk through the door.

"Damn, Mr. Richard, why are you acting like you don't know what I like?"

Mr. Rich was an old retired police officer who took up bartending just to keep his eyes on young women as they came in to have a few drinks. He worked alongside Clarence's dad on the police force.

"Ok, son. Let me get that bud light ready for you, nice and cold."

Clarence took a seat. Mr. Rich slid an ice cold beer down to Clarence, and he hurried and turned his attention to two women who made their way to the bar. After about five minutes of drinking his beer, somebody came in and put their hand on his shoulder. Clarence turned around slowly to see his friend and ex roommate Jason standing behind him.

"What's going on, brother?" Jason said with a nervous tone to his voice. Not knowing the kind of reaction he'd get from Clarence.

"What's going on, bro?"

Clarence said as they gave each other a five, and then a quick hug. Both trying not to be seen hugging by the women sitting at the bar. They both sat down. Mr. Rich saw Jason come in and slid another beer down by them and again began talking with the young women.

"Where you been, man?" Jason asked as he took a sip from his beer.

"I got me an apartment on the other side of town, I needed to be away. I needed to clear my head."

He then took a sip from his beer.

"I understand, bro, I really do, and I wanted to apologize to you about the whole situation with Ashley. I know you really like her, and she's a good girl. But you shouldn't be mad at her because she wanted to tell you, but I was the one who told her I'd tell you considering we're best friends, and I've known you for so long."

He put his beer down on the bar.

"J, it's cool, man. I'm not even thinking about that situation anymore. I've prayed about it, and I've been able to move on from it."

"MY MAN!"

Jason yelled out as they again gave each other a five.

"So, let me ask you, Clarence, have you slept with her yet?" Clarence laughed.

"That's not a conversation we're about to have right now."

Clarence's phone began to vibrate. It was a text message from Ashley.

"Call me ASAP. We need to talk." Clarence quickly stood to his feet.

"Give me a second, bro; I have to make a phone call."

He ran outside. Jason noticed Mr. Rich down on the other end of the bar flirting with the group of women, so he made his way to see if he could join in. Clarence made his way outside and called Ashley.

"Hey, Ashley, what's wrong?" There was a short silence, and then she responded with:

"I'm pregnant."

"Pregnant? Are you sure?" Clarence asked as he rubbed his head.

"Well, I took three tests, and they all said positive, but I set up a doctor's appointment on Monday."

Clarence let out a deep sigh.

"What's wrong, Clarence? What are you thinking?" Clarence cleared his throat before he spoke.

"I'm excited, actually."

This was surprising to Ashley; she didn't know what to say. Seeing how most guys don't get overly excited when they find out that they're going to be a father. So, when a guy says he's excited about becoming a first time father, it's a little surprising.

"Really, Clarence, you're not scared or mad?" He chuckled.

"I'm not scared at all, and why would I be mad? A baby is a blessing from God."

Ashley's smile was so big; he could feel it through the phone.

"I'm going to come over and see you, just let me go pay my tab at the bar."

Clarence then ran back inside with his wallet in his hand. Jason turned and saw how quick he was moving, and he got up and walked to him. And so did Mr. Rich.

"Clarence, what's going on? Why you moving so damn fast, do I need to get my gun?"

Mr. Rich yelled out and began reaching for his pistol that was underneath the bar.

"No, Mr. Rich, calm down. I just got some good news, and I have to go. So, how much do I owe you?" Mr. Rich took his hand off his gun.

"What kinda good news? Boy, only good news that make me move that fast is if my lady calls me and tell me she got some pussy on the plate."

Clarence and Jason both burst out laughing.

"That's crazy, Mr. Rich, but no. my girl just called and told me she's pregnant"

Mr. Rich and Jason's face both lit up.

"Pregnant? Boy, you don't owe Mr. Rich a dime. You gone home and lay up in that pregnant pussy. Pregnant pussy is warmer than grandma's oatmeal on a Sunday morning."

Again, they burst out laughing.

"You sure man?"

He put his wallet back into his pants.

"Boy, if you don't get out of here, I'm gone go lay up with that woman, shit."

Clarence turned to walk out the door, but then Jason grabbed his shirt and spun him around.

"Congrats, brother, I'm happy for you"

They both hugged.

"Thanks, man. I'll call you later and let you know what's going on."

Clarence ran out of the bar to his car. Jason turned around back to the bar to face Mr. Rich.

"Now, you know you gone have to pay his tab, right, boy?"

Mr. Rich held out his hand. Jason laughed.

"Ok, Mr. Rich, here you go."

He paid his tab and Clarence's and even left a tip. Jason then left the bar and made his way to his car. He sat in the car and made a phone call. The phone rang a couple times and then a woman answered.

"Hello, Jason, why are you calling me so late?"

"I'm on my way to your house. We need to talk." He hung up the phone and drove out of the parking lot. Once he reached his destination, he had his door open before he even put the car in park. He ran to the door and knocked. Brittany then opened the door with a robe on and a scarf on her head.

"This better be really important, Jason" She opened the door wide enough for him to make his way through.

"Brittany, Ashley is pregnant." She gasped.

"Oh my God really, wait how do you know that?"

"Because she called Clarence and told him, and then he told me" Jason made his way to the sofa and sat down. Brittany ran to grab her cell phone.

"Where did you see Clarence? I thought he disappeared off the face of earth" She sat next to him on the sofa.

"I went to the bar after work to get a drink, and he was there."

Oh my, God. I have to call my girl. I can't believe she didn't tell me."

"Wait, Brittany, I thought you were mad at her?" She gave him an evil look.

"No sir, I'm mad at your trifling ass. That's my sister." She then began scrolling through her contacts, and then he snatched the phone from her.

"Don't call her, there's something I need to tell you." She leaned back and shook her head.

"You better tell me you gone pay my phone bill; thinking you gone come in here and snatch the phone from me like you've lost your mind." She tried to grab the phone but couldn't reach it, as he held it behind the couch.

"The baby isn't Clarence's it's mine, Brittany." Brittany sat there in shock and her mouth dropped to the floor. "

"What the hell do you mean it's your baby?" Brittany stood to her feet. Before Jason could answer, her phone began to ring. He looked at the phone.

"It's Ashley." Brittany snatched the phone from him.

"Give me my damn phone, and you stay quiet." She then answered it right before it made it to her voicemail.

"Hey, Ashley, what's going on? It's late are you ok?" Ashley didn't respond right away. It took her a few seconds.

"Brittany, I'm pregnant." She sounded more sad than happy when she told her friend.

"Oh my, God. Ashley, are you serious by wh... I mean, uhh." She had to catch herself before she said the wrong thing.

"I told Clarence already. He's on his way to come see me." There was a slight pause between the two of them. Brittany stared at Jason the whole time she was on the phone.

"How does he feel about it?" But before Ashley could respond Brittany asked another question. Trying to make it seem like she didn't already know.

"Wait a minute girl when did you and Clarence hook back up I thought Clarence moved out of state or something" Brittany sat down on the love seat still staring at Jason. Who sat on the sofa with a stale look on his face.

"Who said he moved out of state? I mean, he moved, but he only moved to the other side of town. And one night he and I went to a bar and talked; he invited me to his place, and we had sex. Oh my, God. Brittany, I feel so stupid." Again, there was silence for a few seconds between the two of them.

"Why do you feel stupid?" She stood up and walked to the kitchen and poured herself a glass of wine.

"Do you plan on keeping it?"

"Of course, I'm going to keep it; you know I don't believe in abortions." Brittany took a few sips from her glass.

"Ok, so what's the problem then, it's not like you got pregnant by some low down asshole." That caused Jason to look directly at her. They locked eyes both looking disgusted. Jason was more disgusted with himself than anything.

"I know Clarence is a great guy, and I know he'll be a great father; it's just everything happened so quickly. I never wanted to have a child out of wedlock, you know."

"I understand, Ashley, but just take it as a lesson learned and be the best mother you can be." She placed her glass of wine on the table. Ashley then heard a knock at her door.

"Hey, Brittany, I have to go. Clarence is here, I'll call you tomorrow." She hung up before Brittany could even respond. As soon as she opened the door to let Clarence in, he kissed her and gave her a big hug.

Meanwhile, back at Brittany's apartment, she sat on the love seat just staring at him.

"Ok, Brittany, just let me explain." He sat up on the sofa and turned to face her.

"Jason you lied to me, not only did you lie to me but you lied to your best friend"

"Wait, I didn't lie, when you guys found out about me and Ashley, we had never had sex. I promise." He scooted closer to her and tried to place his hand on her leg, but she moved it before he could.

"She was really going through it after everything came out, and I went to talk to her one night. We had a few drinks and we wound up having sex." Brittany shook her head in disbelief.

"Only thing is, I don't think she remembers. I mean, she was so drunk, it's like she just blacked out." That caused Brittany to jump from her seat.

"Wait a minute are you telling me you raped my friend? I'm calling the cops right now!" He then stood up.

"Hell no, I didn't rape her. She knew what she was doing, but during the sex, it's like she just passed out, and I stopped and went home." Again, this brought a look of disgust to her face.

"You took advantage of my friend while she was down and out and drunk. You knew she was vulnerable, and you slept with her. You're a fuckin asshole, get out of my house." She began walking to the door.

"Brittany, I'm sorry I messed up big time, I know I did. But you can't tell Clarence. I mean, what if it's really his? What if it isn't mine? If he finds this out, he's going to kill me." Brittany placed her hands over her face.

"Jason, either you tell him or I will. Now, get out of my house and don't ever contact me again." Jason walked outside and turned to apologize once again, but she slammed the door in his face.

10

Back at Ashley's place, she and Clarence sat on the sofa and began to discuss her being pregnant.

"What's wrong, Ashley? Why do you look so sad?" Ashley began to cry.

"Clarence, I don't want you to get the wrong idea, but I never wanted to have a child and not be married. I'm an old fashioned kind of woman, I believe in family so much." Clarence began to wipe the tears from her face, and then he pulled her close to him and kissed her forehead.

"Ashley, are you saying you don't want to keep the baby?"

"No, Clarence, I'm not saying that. I'm just saying I wish I could have been married before I had my first child. I mean, what if things don't work out I'm going to be a single mother struggling trying to raise a child by myself. He leaned back, and she turned to face him.

"Did you make this child on your own, Ashley? No you didn't, I played just as much of a part as you, so you'll never be alone when it comes to raising a child that has my blood in their veins." He then grabbed her hand.

"Don't beat yourself up over this. God has a plan for us both, and I'm one hundred percent sure that it's going to all turn out positive, believe me." She smirked just a little as the tears continued to fall from her face.

"All guys say they're going to be around, but as soon as the baby comes out, they turn up missing."

"Well, you trusted me enough to have unprotected sex with me, so I'm asking you to trust me when I say that everything will be ok; just keep the faith." He kissed her lips, and she smiled.

"Speaking of faith, let's pray together and thank God for this blessing." He grabbed her by the hand and said a long prayer.

Afterwards, they both stood up and made their way into her bedroom and laid together listening to the radio. The whole night, Ashley just sat there and watched Clarence as he slept. She knew deep down inside, she had a good man by her side, and after the prayer, she felt even better about their future together. There was only one problem. That night with Jason was a night she couldn't even remember. She didn't even remember having sex with him. Only two people knew of that secret. Jason and Brittany. Ashley finally fell asleep and slept maybe about three of four hours. She woke and heard Clarence coming out of the restroom. He walked out the restroom with his shirt off. Ashley was easily turned on when she saw him without a shirt on. Clarence often worked out. His job was very demanding physically, so it was only right that he stayed in good shape.

"Clarence, you can't walk around here with your shirt off like that you know my hormones are going to be out of control for a while now" Clarence laughed and laid on the bed.

"Oh, is that right, Ashley? Well, in that case, whenever I'm here, I'll never wear a shirt." They both laughed. He leaned towards her and kissed her.

"Oh no, sir, none of that. I have to go to work, and I can't be late again." He leaned back.

"I was thinking maybe you should take the day off today." She gave him a confused look.

"Clarence, I can't take off..." Before she could finish her sentence, he kissed her again.

"Call your job right now, and tell them you're sick. I want to spend the day with you." He stood up and began to put on his shirt.

"Ok, if you say so, sir." She called her job and gave them an excuse.

"I have to go home and change, so I'll be back in an hour. Get dressed and wear something comfortable." She said ok to Clarence as he walked out the door. Within the next hour, Ashley still wasn't ready by the time Clarence made his way back to her apartment. He knocked on the door, and she yelled out,

"IT'S OPEN!" So, he walked in.

"Ashley, are you ready? Let's go."

"Give me a minute, Clarence; I'm putting on my makeup." He made his way to her bathroom.

"You don't have to wear any make up, Ashley, not with me." She smiled.

"Clarence, I want to look nice for you." They both looked at each other and smiled. He walked up to her as she worked on her make up.

"Listen to me, Ashley, no matter how you look or what you're wearing, or how much make up you have on, you will always look good to me." He wrapped his arms around her waist and kissed her neck.

"Now hurry up, woman. Let's go." She smiled as he kissed her neck.

"Ok, Clarence, where are we going?" He pulled away from her and walked into her bedroom.

"Don't worry all you have to do is sit back and ride." Once she finished her makeup, they both made their way to his car. Clarence opened her door, which brought such a big smile to her face. Ashley was not used to a guy like Clarence, so everything seemed so brand new to her. It seemed too good to be true, but it was. As they drove, he grabbed a hold of her hand and kissed it. She turned to look at him as he focused on the road and could do nothing but smile. Then, she looked up to the sky and mouthed,

"Thank you, God." They pulled up to a park which happened to be empty. Not a soul in sight.

"Clarence, what are we doing here?" He didn't answer. He just held out his hand and told her to follow him. They made their way to a table which had flowers and a couple of picnic baskets. There was a guy standing right next to the table. That guy just so happened to be Mr. Rich, the bartender.

"I just wanted to bring you somewhere we could be alone." He walked her to the table and let her sit down first. Then he shook Mr. Rich hand and said thank you. Mr. Rich was responsible for getting things set up while Clarence was away picking up Ashley. Clarence took his seat and Mr. Rich walked off.

"Ashley before we eat do you mind if I tell you something?"

"Of course, Clarence, you can tell me anything." He then grabbed her hand.

"Remember the other day when you asked me if I believed in love at first sight?" She nodded her head.

"Well, I didn't know if I did at first, but I knew when I first saw you that we would have something special. I knew that eventually I would fall in love with you." Ashley's eyes began to water.

"I know what I'm saying right now may not make much sense, but love never does." They both smiled at each other.

Just as Clarence began to finish, his phone rang. It was Jason. He ignored the call. Just a few seconds after, he ignored the call he received a text message from Jason which said.

"Clarence, please give me a call, we really need to talk. This is important." Clarence then turned off his phone.

"So, Ashley what do you think we're going to have?" He moved from his seat across from her to sit next to her.

"Uhh hopefully a boy but as long as the baby is healthy I'll be happy no matter the gender" Clarence placed his arm on her shoulders and pulled her closer to him.

"I'm hoping it's a girl. I've always dreamed of having a daughter." She turned so she could look him in the eyes.

"Really? Most guys usually want their first child to be a boy. Why do you want a girl so bad?"

"I really feel like having a daughter can show me how to really love a woman. I want to have a bond with her that can't be broken. I want to show her how a man is supposed to be, you know what I mean? I think it's easier for a man to raise a boy, but it's more of a challenge to raise a girl." Again, Clarence's words amazed Ashley, and all she could do was smile. Things just seemed too perfect for her. She finally found a man. Not just a man of age, but a real man. She was falling for him. Falling hard. It became evident. She wasn't alone though because Clarence was falling for her as well.

"Clarence, you are truly amazing, how is it that somebody didn't snatch you up before?" He moved his arm off her shoulder.

"Well I've always been the type to run away from relationships. I never really felt like I was ready, but there's something about you that brings something different out of me being around you I feel like everything is just right"

"Stop it Clarence you're going to make me cry" She was too late the tears began to fall down her face.

"What makes you cry whenever we talk? Are you afraid of me Ashley?" He wiped the few tears from her face.

"Actually, I am I mean I'm so used to being let down. The men of my past all let me down, and I can't seem to understand why because I've always given my all, and they just took me for granted, so it's so hard for me to trust anything that a man says."

"Well remember, I told you don't trust what I say, Ashley, trust what I do. And if you don't believe in me, at least believe that God won't let you down unless you allow him into your relationships, then it won't work." Clarence's spiritual side always brought so much emotion out of Ashley. They hugged, and then shared another kiss. Clarence and Ashley spent about another hour at the park, and then made their way back to Ashley's apartment. The sun had gone down already. They pulled inside her complex, and Clarence parked the car. Before opening her door, he stopped her.

"Wait." he hurried and jumped out the car and raced to her side to open the door. Then, he helped her get out of the car. This caused Ashley to laugh.

"Clarence, you don't have to treat me like I'm nine months pregnant. I can get out on my own." He snickered as she made her way out of the car.

"I'm just getting my practice in." He closed her door, and they made their way to her apartment. As they walked through the door, Clarence turned his cell phone on, and it just began to vibrate nonstop.

"I'm going to jump in the shower ok, Clarence?" Clarence sat down on the sofa.

"Yeah, I'll just wait out here for you." She then made her way into the restroom and turned on the water. Clarence scrolled through all the text messages which happened to be from Jason. All of the messages said the same thing.

"Clarence, call me we really need to talk it's important" So, Clarence called Jason. The phone rang twice, and then Jason picked up.

"Clarence, where you at man?"

"I'm out, Jason, what's going on?" Jason didn't respond right away.

"Man, I've been trying to reach you all day. We need to talk." Clarence stood to his feet and walked into the kitchen to make himself a drink.

"Ok, well, talk to me, brother. What's the problem?" Again Jason took a while to respond.

"Man, I don't know where to start."

"I think its best you start from the beginning, man." Jason let out a deep sigh and placed the phone against his chest.

"Clarence, it's about the baby." Clarence took a sip from the dark liquor he had poured into his glass.

"Wait a minute Jason what about the baby?" A long silence occurred.

"Clarence the baby" He paused yet again.

"Clarence the baby is". Jason paused yet again.

"J, what the hell, bro, say what the hell you have to say. Stop hesitating, I'm kinda in the middle of something." Jason cleared his throat. On the other end of the phone, he had sweat dripping from his face. His hands were clammy.

"The baby is going to need a God father, Clarence." Clarence pulled the phone away from his ear and looked at it as if he could actually see Jason.

"Man, I'm going to whoop your ass when I see you Jason why couldn't you just say that?" Clarence laughed. Not knowing that Jason wasn't being completely honest with him. How could he keep such a thing from a guy he's known practically his whole life?

"Well, Clarence I didn't know how you would react to it. I mean, we haven't been on the best of terms considering everything that's happened between me..."

"Man, don't worry about any of that, J, we're brothers. You're like family to me; I'm over all of that stuff from the past." Jason wiped the sweat from his face with his shirt.

"I think that's a pretty good idea though, man, I'm actually at Ashley's place right now. I'm going to run that by her and see what she thinks, and I'll call you tomorrow and let you know."

"Thanks, Clarence; it would definitely be a pleasure to play a big role in your child's life. I mean he or she can just call me 'Uncle J'." Jason then let out a nervous laugh. On the other end of the phone, Clarence had a smile on his face. Clarence, completely unaware of the truth, walked to the sink in the kitchen to put his glass in it.

"Sounds good to me, J, let me get going though, man. I'll call you later."

"Wait, Clarence, before you hang up, there's something else I need to tell you." This time, he didn't hesitate like he did when they first got on the phone.

"Congrats, brother, I'm proud of you, and I'm happy you've found you a great woman like Ashley. You're a lucky man." He then hung up the phone before Clarence could say thank you. Clarence took his phone and put it in his pocket. Out walked Ashley from her bedroom with a towel wrapped around her upper body and another towel wrapped around her head.

"Who was that on the phone, baby?" She asked as she made her way into the kitchen.

"Oh that was Jason; he called to ask if he could be our child's God father." He grabbed Ashley by the hand.

"What do you think of that idea?"

"I mean, Clarence, if that's something you feel will be a good idea, then I don't see why not. I mean, who else would it be, you've been best friends with that man your whole life." Ashley showed no signs of hesitation the way Jason did. Only because the night they shared was not a night she could remember at all.

"Only thing is, he seemed like he was afraid to ask me; that was weird. I mean, I've never known Jason to be one to bite his tongue." Ashley pulled her hand from Clarence.

"Well, speaking of tongue." She stopped and pulled the towel away from her body and stood there completely naked. Clarence didn't even think twice; he pulled her close to him and kissed her. He then picked her up and walked her into the bedroom, and they began to make love.

11

Jason couldn't sit in the house, he needed advice. He needed to clear his mind. So, he went to the place where he knew he could get both. He walked into the bar to see Mr. Rich talking to a young lady. Before he could even make his way to the bar, Mr. Rich called out to him.

"Jason, you ol dry dick muthafucka, what you doing out this late? Ain't it past your bedtime?" Jason barely cracked a smile. Mr. Rich could sense that something was wrong so he turned his attention to the young lady.

"Uhh, excuse me honey, let me talk to my friend here, and I'll get back to you in just a second." He began to walk away but quickly turned back to her.

"But don't you go nowhere, baby girl, its some tricks I want to show you with this bottle here." The woman laughed. Jason then sat down at the other end of the bar.

"What's going on, son, you look nervous like you just got caught sleeping with your best friend's old lady." Jason's eyes lit up. He was even more nervous than before. Only, Mr. Rich was just being his normal self. He had no idea of Jason's secret.

"I'm just messing with you, boy, what's going on?" He cracked open a beer and handed it to Jason.

"Mr. Rich, what would you do if you had a secret that you had to tell someone close to you, but you didn't know how to tell them because it's something that could kill your relationship with that person?" Mr. Rich turned his head to the side. He could sense that something was truly bothering Jason. Jason wasn't being his normal self. Usually he was smiling big and laughing. This was a different side of him.

"Well Jason no matter how good or bad the situation is, I would have to tell them. You know Mr. Rich don't like to keep no secrets." Jason continued to drink his beer. His hands were shaking and still clammy like they were when he was on the phone with Clarence.

"You have to be honest with yourself first, son, then you have to tell the truth to whoever that person is or else you're going to live with that shit on your heart." Jason stood from the bar and pulled a ten dollar bill out of his pocket. He placed it on the bar.

"Thanks, Mr. Rich I really needed to hear that." He then turned around and began to walk away.

"Jason" Mr. Rich called out.

"Remember, son, be honest with yourself first." Jason nodded his head, and then walked out of the bar. Mr. Rich then made his way back to the young lady.

"Now, baby girl, have you ever been with an older man like me?" The woman shook her head.

"Now, don't let these gray hairs fool you, baby girl, Mr. Rich can still move like a young soldier in Vietnam." They both laughed.

Outside, Jason, sat in his car. He just shook his head. Disgusted with himself. He pulled out his cell phone and scrolled through his contacts until he reached Clarence's name. He called him and then hung up before it could even ring. He closed his eyes and shook his head again.

"I can't do this shit." He then drove out of the parking lot.

The next morning, after Clarence left for work, Ashley began to clean up her apartment. Her phone began to ring. It was Brittany.

"Hey, Brittany, what's up?"

"Ashley, we need to talk, are you at home?" Ashley walked from her bathroom into the bedroom and sat on the bed.

"Yes, I'm at home what's up?"

"We need to talk face to face. I'm on my way over there." They hung up.

About an hour later, Brittany was at her door. She knocked a few times, but Ashley couldn't hear her at first because she had the music up loud. So, she called her cell phone to let her know that she was outside. Ashley opened the door, and Brittany stormed into their apartment.

"Brittany, what's wrong?" Brittany took her purse and jacket off and laid them on the sofa.

"How could you lie to me, Ashley, we've been friends for so long? I love you like a sister, and you lied to me." Ashley stood there with a confused look on her face.

"Wait, slow down, what exactly are you talking about what lie are you speaking of I never told you a lie" Brittany walked into the kitchen and Ashley followed behind her. She then grabbed a bottle of wine and a glass and began to pour herself a drink. Before she responded to Ashley she took a couple sips hoping to ease her mind.

"You told me that you and Jason only went on a couple dates and that was it"

"That was it, Brittany, just two dates; nothing more than that." Brittany continued to drink the wine until the glass was completely empty.

"What's really going on? Brittany, is that really why you came over here to ask me about Jason?" Brittany took the glass and dropped it into the sink. Almost breaking it. Brittany took a deep breath. She didn't want to lose her composure. The woman she was speaking to was her best friend and pregnant.

"Jason told me that your baby is his, and it's not Clarence's child." Ashley's mouth dropped.

"Oh my, God, are you serious?" She couldn't believe it. All she could do was stand there and shake her head.

"Why the hell would he tell you that, how could my baby be his? Me and him have never had sex, we've never even kissed." They both stood there silent for a minute or two just staring at each other.

"This is not making any sense, Ashley, why would he say that? What would make him come out and say that he's the father of his best friend's child, that's just crazy." Ashley went and sat on the sofa.

"I can't believe this, Brittany, I really can't, and just last night he asked Clarence to be the baby's God father. I don't understand this." Brittany sat next to her on the sofa.

"We need to get Jason over here, and somebody needs to start telling the truth." She pulled her phone out of her purse and called Jason.

"Hello, Jason where are you?" Jason was surprised to get a call from Brittany. Especially since the last time they were together, she told him to never contact her again.

69

"I just left the gym, why what's up?" He was thinking maybe she was calling him for an early morning fling.

"Don't get the wrong idea, we need to talk—you, me, and Ashley" Jason paused for a second.

"Uhh, what do you mean we need to talk?"

"Jason, don't play stupid. Now, come to Ashley's apartment. I'm sure you know where it is." She then hung up the phone, and threw it back into her purse. Then, she turned her attention to Ashley.

"So, he called Clarence last night and asked to be the God father, but he told me that he's actually the father." They both shook their heads.

"This is crazy, Ashley, somebody is lying, and this is not something you lie about how could you two lie about a child? How could you two lie to your best friends?" Ashley continued to shake her head.

"I don't know what's going on Brittany but I've never slept with that man I never even wanted to"

They both sat there for about another 45 minutes until they heard a knock at the door. Ashley began to get up to answer but Brittany jumped up and told her to sit back down. She went and slung the door open. Not even looking through the peep hole to make sure it was Jason. It was though.

"Don't just stand there dam nit bring your ass inside" Jason made his way into the apartment. Ashley, filled with anger, just stared him down.

"Why in the hell did you tell her that my baby is yours; you know damn well we've never slept together!" Jason stood there in shock. He thought that Brittany would give him a chance to bring this situation up, but of course, she didn't. That's just how women are. Once they're upset, they can't hold water.

"Ashley, do you remember that night I saw you in the bar and we sat there and talked for hours?"

"Yes I do remember that night so the hell what?" Jason began rubbing his head.

"Well you were really drunk and when you made it home you called me and asked me to come over because you didn't want to be alone I didn't think much of it because I knew you were lonely I didn't plan on us having sex but we did" Again Ashley's mouth dropped to the floor.

"Are you fuckin kidding me do you really think that I was that drunk Jason?" He nodded his head.

"No I was not that drunk and no we did not have sex, but yes I did call you once I made it home and that was because my shower wouldn't come on and I asked you to fix it" Jason continued to rub his head.

"Why would you even lie and say we had sex after you fixed my shower you asked could you make yourself a drink and I said ok I'm going to jump in the shower and by the time I got out of the shower you were gone" Brittany turned her attention to Jason waiting for him to respond.

"You're right but I came back and the door was still unlocked I left my wallet in your bathroom, so I came in, and I saw you laying on the bed. At first, I thought you were sleeping, but you called out my name and asked me to lay with you for a little while. At first, I didn't want to, but you kept insisting, so eventually, I gave in." Ashley just stood still

71

and shook her head. Brittany, at a complete loss for words, just stood there not knowing who to believe.

"Jason, stop telling these lies. We didn't have sex. I find it real funny that you're trying to make it seem as if I was drunk out of my mind, but I remember that night like it was yesterday." As she began to speak more, her phone rang. It was Clarence. She quickly answered it.

"Hey, baby, what are you doing? I'm on my lunch break, and I wanted to hear your voice. I sure hope you haven't been on your feet all morning." Ashley tried to smile, but at the moment, she couldn't.

"Oh no, baby, I'm just here talking to Brittany, and stop worrying about me being on my feet all the time. I'm just fine." Clarence laughed.

"But Clarence you and me really need to talk" She stared at Jason as she spoke on the phone. Not trying to let her voice sound angry because she didn't want to upset Clarence while he was at work.

"So as soon as you get off Clarence please come over"

"Ok baby what's wrong" She tried her best to downplay the situation for the moment.

"Oh nothing major, sweetheart, just a few things I feel we need to get for the baby. I didn't want to go out and get them first. I wanted to do it with you there."

"Oh ok, sweetheart, I'll be there when I get off." They then hung up the phone. She stood silent trying to think of what to say next but before she could Jason spoke.

"Ashley you can't tell Clarence about this he's going to be so pissed off there's no telling what he'll do this will break his heart"

"What the hell do you mean I can't tell him? Oh no I'm going to tell him as soon as he walks through that door" She walked over to the door.

"And speaking of the door here it is now please get the hell out; I don't ever want you to come by here again." She opened the door. Jason had nothing more to say so he walked outside without saying a word.

"And don't even think about being the God father, I don't ever want you to see my child." She slammed the door. Then she turned her attention to Brittany.

"Brittany, I swear to you, he's lying. Everything I just said was the truth, and the only reason I even called him to help me with the shower was because Clarence wasn't speaking to me, and I didn't want to have to pay to get it fixed." Brittany walked up to Ashley and gave her a hug.

"It's ok, Ashley, I believe you, but whatever you do, don't tell Clarence." Ashley pulled away from her.

"What do you mean, Brittany? I have to tell him his best friend has lied and said that he slept with me, and I'm carrying his child, and he even wants him to be the God father."

"I know, Ashley, but you know that you guys didn't sleep together, so just don't tell him; just tell him you don't want Jason to be the God father. I mean, make something up, but don't tell him the real reason why. He may get so upset and hurt Jason, and then you're going to be alone raising that child."

Ashley began to shake her head. She didn't know what to do. She knew that if she told Clarence, it would break his heart, and at the same time, upset him so much that he might even kill Jason. If it led to that, then she'd be stuck with a newborn all by herself. Brittany left just a little after Jason. Ashley just sat there on the couch confused. She was torn. The idea of telling Clarence and what he would do to Jason just began to eat her up inside. But how could she keep such a thing from the father of her child? She thought that maybe if she just tried to move on from it, then it would all just blow away. But how could that even be possible? Jason wanted to be the God father of the child.

12

Once Clarence got off work, he jumped in his car and began to drive to Ashley's apartment. He pulled out his cell phone to call her and let her know that he was on the way. When the phone rang, Ashley sat and stared at the screen before she answered it.

"Hey, baby. I didn't think you'd pick up. I thought maybe I'd have to leave a voicemail." He snickered. Ashley didn't speak.

"Umm, hello? Ashley, are you there?" He could hear her breathing and figured that something was wrong.

"Yes, Jason, I'm fine." Her emotions were so up and down at the moment, she didn't even realize that she called him Jason.

"JASON!" Clarence shouted out.

"Clarence, why are you yelling at me?"

"Ashley, you just called me, Jason." She then took the phone and placed it against her chest and slapped her hand on her forehead.

"No, Clarence I didn't call you, Jason."

"Ok, well whatever, I'll talk to you later." She let out a deep sigh.

"Clarence, I'm serious don't act like that. I have a lot on my mind. I really need to talk to you." Clarence didn't respond.

"Clarence, I'm sorry. Jason just left."

"What the hell was he doing over there?" Before she could respond, he yelled again,

"HELLO, DAMNIT! WHAT WAS HE DOING AT YOUR FUCKING APARTMENT?" This was not like Clarence. He was very laid back. He didn't normally get upset, and when he would get upset he would get quiet and not say much.

"Clarence, he was here with Brittany they both just left." Again, Clarence was silent. He realized how upset he was getting, and he didn't want to say the wrong thing. Knowing that Ashley was pregnant, and he didn't want to anger her or stress her any more.

"Clarence, can you please just come talk to me? I don't really feel good I've been having heart burn all day."

"Ok, Ashley, I'm on the way."

He stopped at a gas station close to her apartment and got himself a beer. Beer seemed to help Clarence ease his mind a little. He needed to do that before he got to her place because he didn't want to blow things up not knowing what was actually going on. He made it to her apartment and tossed the beer can on the ground. As soon as he made his way to the stairs his cell phone began to ring. It was Jason.

"Hello." Clarence answered in a serious tone.

"Clarence, what's going on, brother? I really need to talk to you, man."

"Well, I'm kinda in the middle of something, so I'm gone have to call you back."

Before he could hang up, Jason screamed out, "Wait, Clarence, it's about the baby!" Clarence pulled the phone from his ear and began to hang it up, but before he did placed it back on his ear.

"Jason, I don't have time for this shit right now."

"Clarence, I don't think it's a good idea for me to be the child's God father, I plan on moving out of state. I mean, what kind of God father would I be if I'm never around, ya know?"

He hung up before Clarence could even respond. Clarence thought about calling him back, but he had other issues to tend to which were more important. He put his cell phone in his pocket hand jogged up the steps. Clarence knocked a few times and Ashley opened it. She was fresh out of the shower so she had on her robe and a towel around her head.

"Baby, first off, let me apologize for yelling at you. I had a real long day at work." He grabbed her, and then kissed her forehead.

"It's ok, Clarence, but I have to talk to you about Jason."

"You know what, baby, he just called me and told me he didn't want to be the baby's God father because he's moving out of state; that was a little weird to me." He made his way into the living room. Before he sat down he turned to her.

"So, what were you going to say?" She stood there with a confused look on her face.

"He said the same exact thing to me." Ashley couldn't find it in her heart to tell Clarence the truth. She was afraid of how he would react. So, she kept what really happened to herself.

"Really, I wonder why?" He motioned her to come and sit next to him on the sofa and she did.

"That just makes no sense. I mean, for one, why would he just up and leave, and two, why would he say he didn't want to be the God father?" Ashley just sat there shaking her head.

"I don't know, Clarence, it's crazy to me." Clarence began to shake his head, and then he stood to his feet.

"Oh well, forget it. I'll call him later maybe he's just going through something. Go get dressed baby, let's go get something to eat. I know you're hungry." He laughed, but Ashley who had begun to gain the weight from the baby didn't find it funny at all.

"Are you calling me fat, Clarence?" Clarence cracked a smile.

"No, baby, not at all. I just figured you were... Man, never mind. Just get dressed, and let's go out." Ashley then went into the bedroom to get dressed. She heard her phone going off. It was a text message from an unknown number.

"I'm sorry," read the message. She put the phone down as she heard Clarence come into the room. The phone vibrated again.

"Come on, woman. I'm starving, you don't have to get all dolled up; just throw on some sweats."

"Ok, Clarence, I'm coming." Clarence walked out of the room, and she picked the phone up to read what the message said.

"I didn't mean to leave the way I did. I hope that we can work things out. I really enjoyed you." She then began to text back. "Ashley, I'll be waiting in the car." Clarence yelled from the living room. He then walked outside and down to his car. Her text message read:

"JASON, DO NOT CONTACT ME ANYMORE, PLEASE. I DONT KNOW WHAT YOUR PROBLEM IS, BUT IT NEEDS TO STOP. ME AND CLARENCE ARE HAVING A CHILD, AND WE ARE GOING TO BE TOGETHER. HE IS YOUR BESTFRIEND, AND

I AM HIS WOMAN. I NEED FOR YOU TO RESPECT THAT, SO PLEASE STAY OUT OF OUR LIVES."

She then grabbed her jacket and purse and made her way outside the apartment. They pulled up to a steakhouse that Clarence went to alone.

"Don't you even think about opening that door, Ashley." He hurried up and jumped out of the car and opened her door. She shook her head as she climbed out of the car.

"Clarence, I told you I'm not in labor already, you don't have to break your neck just to try and get me out of the car."

"Ashley, I told you I'm getting my practice in." They made their way into the restaurant. They were greeted by a hostess with a big smile on her face.

"Hey, you guys, welcome. Table for two?" They both nodded. She grabbed two menus, and then turned back to them.

"Smoking or non-smoking?"

"Non" Clarence Responded

She then turned and walked them to a booth towards the back of the restaurant. The restaurant was quite empty.

"Here you guys go. My name is Sherri, your waitress' name is Monica, and she'll be with you guy's in just a second." She sat them and placed the menus on the table and walked off.

"Ashley, are you ok? You were quiet the whole ride here, you've been acting strange."

"Oh, I'm fine, Clarence, just a little tired, that's all." He picked up his menu and began to look through it as if he didn't already know what he was going to order. Then, Ashley's phone began to ring. She pulled her phone out of her purse to see it was Brittany. At first she thought about ignoring the call, but she answered anyway.

"Hey Ashley have you talked to Clarence yet?"

"Brittany, I can't talk right now. I'll call you later." before she could hang up, Brittany yelled out.

"Remember, Ashley, don't tell Clarence about..." Ashley hung up the phone before she could finish.

"Everything ok, baby?" Ashley placed her cell phone on the table.

"Yes, Clarence, everything is just fine, baby." Their waitress walked up to the table.

"Hi. My name is Monica; what can I get for you guys to drink?" Clarence ordered a sweet tea, and Ashley water.

"Are you guys ready to order, or do you need more time to look over the menu?"

"Umm, give us a few more minutes." Clarence responded to her. He figured Ashley wasn't ready. She barely even looked at the menu.

"Clarence, I'm going to use the restroom. I'll be right back." She jumped up and grabbed her phone and headed for the restroom.

When she made her way into the restroom, her phone vibrated again. It was from the same unknown number from earlier in the day. The message read

"Jason??? Who Is Jason?"

Ashley stood there in the restroom confused. If it wasn't Jason who was texting her phone, then who could it be? Before she walked out of the restroom, she called the number. It went straight to voicemail. She called it two more times. Same result. So, she went to mirror and looked at herself then turned away and walked out of the restroom. She walked back to the table and saw the waitress talking to Clarence.

"Hey, are you ready to order?" Ashley didn't take her seat she stood next to the waitress and in front of Clarence.

"Clarence, I'm not really hungry anymore, can we just go home?" Clarence stood to his feet.

"What's wrong, baby, is everything ok?"

"I'm just feeling a little light headed, and my stomach is really bothering me. I don't really have much of an appetite." She grabbed her purse and walked outside.

"I'm so sorry; she's not really feeling good how much I owe you for the drinks?" He began to reach in his pocket for his wallet.

"Don't worry about it, sir, the drinks are on the house. I hope your girlfriend feels better though." Clarence put his wallet back in to his pants.

"Thank you so much." He then made his way out the restaurant to see Ashley leaning against his car.

"Are you sure you're ok, baby? I mean, you've been acting strange all day. Talk to me, and tell me what's wrong."

He unlocked the door, and then opened her door. She climbed into the car and Clarence made his way to the driver's seat and the got in. Before he started the engine, he sat there and waited for her to give him a response.

"Clarence, I'm fine. I just don't feel good. I just want to be alone."

Clarence sat still in his seat confused. Wondering what was going on with the woman who was carrying his child. He didn't want to start an argument, so he just started the car, and then drove out of the parking lot. Ashley's phone lit up. Clarence heard the loud vibration, but didn't turn to look; he just stayed focused on the road. She turned the phone over, and there was a text message from the unknown number.

"I'm sorry I missed your call. I'll call you as soon as I get a chance."

She then turned the phone back over to try and act as if what she read was unimportant. The whole ride was a silent. Neither Clarence nor Ashley knew what to say to each other. As soon as they pulled into her apartment, Clarence parked in front of her stairway. He began to unbuckle his seatbelt, but before he could open his door, Ashley stopped him by kissing him on the cheek. She placed her hands on his face and kissed his lips.

"Don't worry, Clarence. I'm ok, I'll just take a nap, and I'll call you as soon as I wake up."

Clarence was at a loss for words, so he just nodded his head. Ashley got out of the car and made her way up the stairs. Clarence waited for her to walk into her apartment, and then he drove off. He needed answers. He didn't know where to start, but he sure had an idea.

13

As soon as Ashley entered her apartment, she called Brittany. The phone rang about three times, and then Brittany finally answered.

"Brittany, I really need to talk to you. Something weird is going on."

"Wait, slow down, girl, tell me what's wrong." Ashley went into her bedroom and sat on the bed.

"Ok, well first, I didn't tell Clarence about Jason, but I've been getting random text messages from an unknown number."

"What kind of text messages, Ashley?"

"Well, whoever it is texting me apologized for something I don't know I can't remember what the text said. I deleted it, but I thought it was Jason."

"Why would you think it was Jason though?" There was a short silence.

"Because of the confusion he's caused with this baby, but I sent him a message back calling him by name thinking that it was actually him telling him to never contact me again"

Ashley was full of mixed emotions, and Brittany could tell. "Ashley, you have to calm down. Slow down and breathe."

"Me and Clarence went out to eat, and I got another text message from that same number asking who Jason is. I have no idea who this is on my phone, but it's really aggravating me."

"Well, did you tell Clarence?"

Again, there was a short silence.

"No, I just told him I wasn't hungry, and I didn't feel good, so he brought me back home. Brittany, I have to tell him. I can't keep lying to him because I saw the hurt in his eyes. This man truly cares about me, and I'm keeping these secrets from him it's not fair."

Brittany let out a long deep sigh.

"I don't know what to tell you, Ashley." They continued to talk on the phone for about another thirty minutes. Meanwhile, Clarence couldn't go home without at least having an idea of what had been going on lately, so the first stop he made was to his old apartment in which he shared with Jason. He parked the car and jumped out. As he made his way up the stairs, he saw a guy walking out and closed the door.

"Excuse me, sir."

Clarence said to the man as they passed each other on the stairs. There was something familiar about the man who he passed on the stairs. Something so familiar, that it made Clarence turn back around to try and take another look at the guy's face. Before he knocked on the door, he stood there wondering where he remembered seeing this man's face. Nothing came to him right away. He then began to knock on the door. But who was this man that Clarence recognized. And what was he doing coming out of Jason's apartment? Clarence knocked at the door a couple times but Jason didn't answer right away. He stood there and waited for a while. He just shook his head wondering where he remembered the guy he just passed on the stairs. Still, nothing came to him. Finally, Jason opened the door.

"Hey, what's going on, Clarence." He held out his hand. Clarence hesitated before he shook it.

"What's wrong man?" Clarence stood with a blank look on his face. Eventually he shook Jason's hand. "Just trying to figure things out, man, everything has been so crazy lately." Jason opened up the door for Clarence to come inside.

"What's going on, Jason, why are you moving out of state, and why don't you want to be the God father anymore?" Jason didn't have an answer for Clarence, so he tried to switch the subject. "How's Ashley?"

"Stop fucking playing around, Jason, I can't deal with the bullshit today. I've had too much of everybody lying to me now, right now, I need answers."

Clarence's aggression surprised Jason. His eyes widened, and his mouth dropped to the floor. "Clarence, sit down, man. I'll tell you what's going on." Clarence shook his head.

"I don't want to sit down, Jason. Now, tell me what's going on" Jason made his way to the sofa and sat down. His hands were sweating from being so nervous. They began to shake as he started talking.

"Ok, Clarence, I just feel like if your child is going to have a God parent, then they should have one who will be able to be around often, and with me being out of state, I won't be able to do that."

"Why the hell are you moving?"

Jason again had no answer.

"So, what do you think you guys are going to have a boy or a..."

"Stop fucking bullshitting me, Jason, I've known you damn near half my life. Why are you being so secretive?" Jason let out a deep sigh.

"Ok, Clarence, here it is. I got into some deep shit with Brittany, ok? I put my hands on her, and now I think she's trying to get the police involved. So, I have to leave before things get crazy."

He couldn't look Clarence in his eyes, because deep down inside, he knew he was lying to his best friend. "You hit her?" Jason nodded his head. "Look, man, please don't tell anybody. I know you're an officer and all, but come on, man. Keep this one silent, man, as my best friend. Please, don't tell anybody that you know."

Clarence stood by the door shaking his head. He could tell his friend wasn't being completely honest with him. "Clarence, I was drunk one night, man, and we were arguing. And I reacted without thinking. I'm not sure if she's going to press any charges, but I need to get away just in case she does."

"Are you telling me the truth, Jason, or is this just some bullshit, cover up story?" Again, Jason nodded his head. "Clarence, I've been knowing you damn near my whole life, you know I've never lied to you." They both stared each other down.

Both knowing that Jason was telling a big lie. A lie that would just add more confusion and more drama to the situation. "Well, I don't want to get into you guy's business, Jason, but you do know that it's going to be hard for me to not say anything. I mean, that is my job." Clarence figured maybe he could try and put a little fear into Jason to try and get him to tell the truth. His plan failed.

"I know, buddy, but I'm just asking you to do me a solid, man. Just help me out, please." Jason stood to his feet and walked towards Clarence. He held out his hand once again. And again, Clarence hesitated before he shook it. When he finally did, he didn't let go as quick as he did when he first got to the apartment.

"Just make sure you're not lying to me, Jason, I would hate to have to get involved." Again, Jason nodded his head. He tried to pull away, but Clarence held on.

"So, you've got you a new roommate already?" He let Jason's hand go.

"New roommate? Who are you talking about?" Clarence shook his head.

"When I first got here, I saw a guy coming down the stairs. He actually looked really familiar, but I can't remember from where."

"Oh, you mean John?" Clarence shrugged his shoulders.

"Yeah, his name is John. He's going to be taking over the apartment for me when I leave. I just met the guy."

"Wait, you just met the guy, and you're going to let him take over the apartment; what kind of sense does that make, Jason?" Jason walked to the kitchen opened the fridge and pulled out a beer. He popped it open and took a sip.

"Yeah, man, I filled the guy out. I talked to him and got to know him. He actually seems like a good guy. He told me he used to live here in the city, but he moved away after him and his ex-broke up, but he was so in love with her that he had to move away. He even said that he saw her at the bar we always go to, but she was with some guy, so she didn't even speak to him."

Clarence froze after he heard those words. He just stared at the wall. It had finally hit him where he knew the guy from.

87

"Clarence, Clarence, CLARENCE!" Jason called out Clarence's name, who just so happened to be stuck in a daze.

"Hey, Jason, I have to go, man. I'll talk to you later."

"Wait, bro, we have to finish…" before he could finish, Clarence had already walked outside and close the door. Clarence left the apartment and jumped in his car. Things were beginning to unfold, and he needed answers. He wasn't the type of guy to jump to conclusions or assume much, but he felt like he was being lied to by everybody around him. He drove back to Ashley's apartment. Clarence chose not to call her, he just showed up unannounced. Once he made it to her apartment, he didn't even park his car straight in the parking spot. He jumped out of the car and ran upstairs and banged on her door. Ashley opened the door after a few knocks. She didn't open the door all the way just enough for her and Clarence to be able to see one another.

"Hey, Clarence, what are you doing here?" Clarence sensed that there was something going on, and he tried to peek into her apartment to see for himself.

"Why are you holding the door like I'm some stranger? Ashley, let me in. We need to talk." He pushed his way into the apartment.

"CLARENCE, WAIT—" Before she could finish a man walked out of her bedroom. It was the same man from the bar. The same man Clarence saw leaving Jason's apartment.

"What the hell is going on?"

"Clarence, before you get mad, it's not what you think. I promise." Clarence stood by the bed in disbelief.

Then, the man spoke out.

"Look, man, it's not what you—" Before he could finish, Clarence walked up to him and stood in his face.

"Before you finish whatever it is you're about to say, I suggest you think about it. As of matter of fact, I think its best you leave before I hurt you." The man wanted no trouble, so he began to walk to the door. He turned back to face Ashley.

"Listen, Ashley, I'm sorry once again. I didn't mean to cause any confusion." Clarence walked to the door and opened it.

"Don't you say another word to her, now GET THE HELL OUT!" He then walked out, and Clarence slammed the door.

"WHAT THE HELL WAS HE DOING HERE, ASHLEY?" Ashley placed her hands over her face. She then moved her hands from her face, and her eyes were full of tears.

"Clarence, he was just here visiting me, that's all."

"That's bullshit, what the hell was he doing in your bedroom?" The tears began to fall from her eyes.

"Clarence, he was using the restroom, that's all. The other restroom isn't working, so I told him he could use that one."

"That's why you didn't want to let me in got here, isn't it?" She could sense that Clarence was angry and probably wouldn't listen to a word she said until he calmed down. Then, there was a knock at the door. Ashley walked to the door to open it.

"Don't you open that damn door, we're talking." She paid no attention to Clarence's demand. She looked through the peep hole, but couldn't tell who it was. So, she opened the door slowly.

"Umm, yes, how may I help you?" On the other side of the door, there was a woman holding her pregnant stomach.

"Hi, I'm John's wife; he left his keys up here. I just came to get them." Clarence stood in the living room confused. It showed in his face. He began to wonder what was really going on.

"Wait, did you say wife?"

"Yes, Clarence, she said wife," Ashley answered for the woman as she grabbed John's keys from the kitchen.

"Thank you, Ashley, and again, it was nice meeting you."

"Likewise, and be careful walking down the steps make sure you tell John I said congrats and you guy's be sure to send lots of pictures of the baby" The woman smiled and walked out of the apartment.

After Ashley closed the door she turned to face Clarence.

"So, what were you saying, Clarence?" The confused look stuck to his face.

"I don't get it, Ashley. Why didn't you want to let me in when I first got here?"

"Because I knew once you saw him, then you'd jump to all kinds of conclusions." She began to walk towards Clarence.

"But you could've just told me what was going on instead of making it seem like you were trying to hide something. I was almost ready to kill that man." He snickered, and then gave her a hug.

"I'm sorry for causing a scene and just popping up, baby. It's just so much going on, I feel so lost." As they hugged Ashley placed her head on his chest.

"Clarence, baby, in order for us to make it you have to trust me."

"I know, baby. I have to do better."

They hugged for a few minutes, and then began to make out. Things were beginning to become very confusing for Clarence. His girlfriend and mother of his unborn child had begun to act very strange. He couldn't tell if she was just having the normal mood swings of a pregnant woman, or if she was keeping something from him. Then, there was Jason. Who was his best friend for years. He all of a sudden wanted to move out of town. Right after he asked to be the child's God father. Then, there was this mysterious guy named John. He just so happened to run into this man three times. This man seemed to be the biggest issue for Clarence. There were so many questions and not enough answers. Clarence left Ashley's house feeling lost, but he couldn't call Jason or even talk to Ashley, because deep down inside, he felt as if both of them were lying to him. So, he decided to go and talk to the person he knew he could count on to be straight forward with him. He went to the bar to talk to Mr. Rich. As soon as he walked into the bar he didn't see Mr. Rich but he sat down at the bar anyways. There was a young lady standing behind the bar with a towel in her hand washing a glass.

"Hey, uhh. Where's Mr. Rich?" The woman placed the glass down on the bar and put the towel over her shoulder.

"He went out back to smoke a cigarette. What can I get for you, handsome?"

"I need something strong and smooth; usually I just drink beer, but I have a lot on my mind. I'm not big on hard liquor. What do you recommend?" The young woman walked away. She came back with two bottles in each hand.

91

"Ok, Hennessy or Remy martin; they're both pretty smooth."

"Which do you prefer?" The woman smiled.

"Well, I don't really drink liquor. I'm more of a wine kinda gal, but if I had to choose, I would go with the Hennessy. It's nice and strong and pretty damn smooth." She placed the Remy martin underneath the bar.

"Ok, well I guess I'll go with Hennessy then, and make it nice and strong, please."

"Would you like coke or anything with it?" Clarence shook his head. She grabbed him a glass and filled it almost to the top.

"Now, take your time with that, since you're not a hard core drinker." Clarence let out a light chuckle.

"Ok, I'll be sure to take it easy." Two guys walked in and sat down at the other end of the bar.

"Let me go take care of these guys, and I'll be back down to check on you." Clarence held up his glass and then took a sip as the woman walked off. Clarence had his head down, and a man came to sit next to him at the bar. The young bartender came back down and asked

"Yes, sir. How may I help you?" This caused Clarence to look up. As the guy began to order, Clarence turned to see who he was, and it just so happened to be John. Once he finished ordering, John turned his attention towards Clarence.

"Hey, how's it going buddy?" John held out his hand for a hand shake.

"It's Charles, isn't it?" Clarence stared at the man, and then shook the guy's hand.

"Clarence." they shook hands for a few seconds, and then let go

"Oh, that's right, Clarence. I'm sorry we haven't been properly introduced." Clarence took another sip from his drink and nodded his head.

"Ashley told me a lot about you." Clarence not being much of a drinker began to feel the alcohol, and he wasn't really in the mood to talk to John, and the frustration showed on his face.

"Oh yeah, and what exactly did she tell you?" The young bartender walked back up with two shot glasses.

"Here you go, sir, two shots of Gin." she placed the shot glasses in front of him and walked off.

"Oh you, know she told me how much she really cares about you, and that she's never met a guy like you." He took down one shot and placed it back on the bar.

"Wait a minute, who exactly are you? I mean, I know nothing about you."

"Me and Ashley used to date a few years back. Things didn't work out between us; I moved away for personal reasons, and now I'm trying to move back, since I've gotten myself back together."

"What about the pregnant woman who came to get your key's the other night? Who was that?" John took down the second shot.

"That was my wife." Clarence looked the man in his eyes. He didn't sense that the man was lying to him.

"So, what about Jason, how do you know him?" Clarence took the last sip of his drink and placed the glass on the bar.

"I don't really know him. I was just looking at his apartment because he was trying to rent it out. I figured it would be a nice place for my wife, our child, and myself until we're able to get a house built." The frustration on Clarence's face began to fade. He felt more at ease.

"But I'm not too sure if we're going to move into the apartment. I'll have to look around some more. Plus, that guy, Jason, seemed a little strange; he seemed really nervous when he was showing me the apartment. I didn't know what to think of it, and he said he really needed to get out as soon as possible. Seemed a little weird to me." John had definitely caught Clarence's attention.

"Hey, John, Hey Clarence what's going on, you two knuckleheads?" Mr. Rich walked in from the back holding a box of cigarettes.

"Hey, what's going on, Mr. Rich? Sorry, I can't stay to talk to you, but I have to get home to my wife." He reached in to his back pocket and began to pull out his wallet.

"Oh, it's alright, son. I understand, but you don't pay me, you pay Melinda. I'm off for the night." John nodded his head and walked to the other end of the bar to pay the woman, and then walked out of the bar.

"Clarence, my main man, what do you think of Melinda?" Clarence sat there in a daze.

"CLARENCE!" Mr. Rich yelled out his name again.

"Yea, Mr. Rich, what's up?"

"I said what do you think of Melinda? My new bartender. I'm getting old, son. I need some help around here. Did she take good care of you?"

94

Clarence nodded his head.

"Oh yeah, she's great."

"Good, that's what I like to hear, did you see the ass on her though? If I wasn't trying to get some good help around here, I'd lay her out on this bar and give it to her like I just finished doing ten years up state." They both laughed.

"How do you know that guy, John?" Mr. Rich was a man known for his good judge of character.

"I've known him since he was a little boy, I grew up with his dad just like I grew up with yours; good to see him back in town, he's a pretty solid guy just like his old man." Again, Clarence began to feel betrayed by a man he called his best friend for years. Clarence sat at the bar until closing time. He didn't order another drink; he just sat there in complete silence. Watching people come and go. He had already paid his tab, and Mr. Rich had left for the night. Melinda, the new bartender, was still behind the bar cleaning up.

"Are you ok, Clarence?" He sat there and stared her down before he responded.

"Yeah, I'm fine. Just got a lot on my mind." She made her way from behind the bar and sat next to him.

"Anything you want to talk about?" He shook his head.

"Oh no, it's ok. I'm just going to go home now, but thanks anyway"

"Hey anytime sweetheart" She stood up and began to walk back behind the bar. Clarence stood up and began to walk out.

"Hey, Clarence." He turned around to face her.

"Go talk to your girl" He gave her a look and wondered how she knew that he had an issue with his woman. She winked at him and walked to the back. Clarence walked outside and jumped into his car. He went home instead of going to talk to Ashley.

14

Meanwhile, at Ashley's apartment.

Ashley had just walked out of her restroom after taking a shower and she heard a knock at her door. She wasn't really expecting any company, so she wasn't sure who it could be. She walked to the front door and looked through the peep hole. She put her head down after seeing who it was.

"Oh, God, what's he doing here?" She whispered to herself. She stood at the door for a few more seconds before she opened it. When she finally did open the door, the man who was knocking began to walk away. She called out to him before he made it to the stairs.

"John." John turned to her as she called out his name.

"Oh hey, Ashley I didn't think you were home" He began to walk back towards the apartment.

"Do you have a minute? I just want to talk." Ashley nodded her head and let him inside.

"So, what's going on, John? What brings you over here?" She took him into the living room, and they both sat down. Ashley sat on the sofa and John on the love seat.

"I ran into Clarence today." Ashley's eyes widened.

"Where did you see him?"

"Down at Mr. Rich's bar."

"Oh, well, did you guy's speak to each other?"

"Yeah, believe it or not we had ourselves a nice little conversation. He asked a lot of questions though; that's the reason I came over." Ashley sat up on the sofa.

"Ashley, is everything ok?" She let out a long deep sigh.

"John, how could you text me and tell me you want to work things out between us, and you're married with a child on the way?"

"Wait, Ashley, what are you talking about?" This made him sit up straight and look her in the eyes.

"A couple of days ago, you sent me a message saying how you enjoyed me, and wish we could work things out. I thought you were somebody else at first, and when I said his name you asked who he was. Come on, John, I know how you do things, don't play crazy." John sat on the love seat shaking his head.

"Uhh, first off, Ashley, I have no idea what text you're talking about. I've never sent you anything like that. You have things confused. That really wasn't me." Ashley looked John into his eyes. Something inside of her made her believe that he was telling the truth.

"So, who did you think it was at first, Ashley?"

"I thought it was Clarence's best friend, Jason." John leaned his head back when he heard Jason's name.

"Jason?" She nodded her head.

"What would make you think it was Jason?"

Ashley dropped her head. She sat there for a few seconds before raising her head. Her eyes began to water. Of course, with her being pregnant her hormones began to take over again. John moved from the love seat to the sofa and sat next to Ashley.

"Jason told my best friend that I'm pregnant with his child. It's just so much mess, John; I don't even want to talk about it."

"Well, what would make him say anything like that? Did you sleep with Ja—" She cut him off.

"Hell no, NEVER!" Ashley yelled out.

"Calm down, Ashley. I mean, this just isn't making any sense to me."

"How do you think I feel, John?" He just sat there and shook his head.

"What about Clarence, does he know about this?"

"No, John, I don't know how to tell him. I'm afraid if I do tell him, then he's going to lose his mind, and he's going to kill Jason. And Jason is trying to move out of town because of all of this." When she said that, John stood to his feet.

"So, that's why he's trying to get somebody to move into his apartment, so quick and that's why he was acting so strange?" John sat back down and placed his hand on her shoulder.

"Listen to me, Ashley, you have to tell Clarence. This isn't something you keep from him." Ashley shook her head.

"I just don't know how."

"Well, you have to figure it out, Ashley, don't let this drag on; it's only going to make things worse. There seems to be a lot of confusion between you guys, and that's not good. Just tell him and maybe he won't do anything to Jason. I mean, who knows, but you can't keep this a secret any longer." He stood up again.

"I have to get home; my wife has been waiting on me." He grabbed Ashley by the hand, and she stood up.

He gave her a big hug and headed towards the door. He opened it, but before he walked out, he turned to Ashley.

"Tell him." John closed the door and headed to his car. The next morning, John made his way to Jason's apartment to talk with him. He didn't call Jason to let him know he was coming, he just showed up. John knocked on the door a few times, and there was no answer. He waited for a few minutes, and there was no answer. As he turned to walk down the stairs, there was Jason standing at the bottom of the steps.

"Hey, what's going on, John, you got some good news for me, man?" Jason was hoping that John had showed up to tell him that he would move into his apartment. The look on John's face showed otherwise.

"Oh, man, umm..." Before he could finish, Jason cut him off.

"Come on, man, let's go inside and talk." Jason walked up the stairs and into the apartment.

"So, man what you got for me?" John stood at the door as Jason made his way into the kitchen.

"You want something to drink?"

"No, I'm good, Jason, I won't be staying long." Jason walked out of the kitchen, and his smile turned upside down.

"What's wrong, John?"

"Jason, I won't be moving into this apartment." They stood in silence for a few seconds.

"Why not? I thought you liked it." John shook his head.

"The apartment is fine, but it's you I have an issue with."

Jason stood with a confused look on his face. He couldn't seem to understand why John seemed so upset all of a sudden. John walked away from the door and stood face to face with Jason.

"I know what the hell is going on, Jason." Jason took a step back.

"Wait. Wait. Wait. What are you talking about, man?" His shoulders flinched, and he held his hands out as he waited for an explanation.

"You know what the hell is going on, you're playing with fire, and I should kick your ass around this apartment right now, but you aren't worth it." Jason still confused just stood shaking his head. He had no idea that Ashley told John about their situation. He had no clue whatsoever.

"You just need to know that karma is a bitch, and it's going to bite you in your ass. I'd much rather you suffer from that, than me whooping your ass. It'll hurt you a lot more." He opened the door and turned to look at Jason, and then left without saying another word. He slammed the door which caused the living room to shake. Jason stood there in a daze.

"What the hell was that?" He said to himself as he stood still in his living room.

Meanwhile, Ashley's morning was being spent trying to figure out how she would break the news to Clarence. She called his phone, and it went straight to voicemail. She put it down on her pillow, and then the phone rang. It was Clarence.

"Hey, baby, open the door. I brought you breakfast."

Ashley was actually shocked. She wasn't expecting to see him this early and she hadn't even come up with how she was going to tell him what had been going on. Her hands were shaking as she made her way to the door. She paused before she opened it to try and regain her composure. She opened the door to see Clarence standing there with a big bag of tacos.

"Hey, baby, I brought you some tacos. I know how much you love these." He walked inside, and Ashley closed the door.

"Umm, Clarence, we really need to talk."

"Ok, baby, let's eat first. I'm starving." He made his way into the living room and sat down. Ashley walked slowly into the room. Clarence pulled a taco out of the bag; he unwrapped it, and began to eat.

"I'm not really hungry right now, Clarence, but there is something I've been wanting to talk to you about. I just didn't know how." Clarence wasn't really paying much attention to her as he continued to stuff his face.

"CLARENCE!" She yelled out to get his attention.

"Yeah, baby, I'm listening. Go ahead." She took a deep breath.

"Well, it's actually about Jason." Clarence pulled the taco away from his mouth. He then placed the taco on the table.

"What about Jason?"

He still had a mouth full of food. Clarence grabbed a napkin from the bag and wiped his mouth. Ashley hesitated to speak.

"WHAT ABOUT JASON?" His tone of voice changed.

"Well, I know the reason he doesn't want to be the baby's God father, and I know why he wants to move away." Clarence sat silent waiting for her to finish. Ashley began to cry. She sat next to Clarence on the sofa and placed her hand on his knee.

"Clarence, I really love you." Clarence pulled his knee from her hand.

"What's going on, Ashley?" She began to cry even harder. Clarence stood to his feet.

"Ashley you need to tell me what the hell is going on" Her whole body began to shake as she tried to force the words to come out.

"Clarence, Jason told Brittany that the baby is his. He told her that we had sex."

"YOU HAD SEX WITH JASON?" Ashley rose to her feet.

"No, Clarence it's all a lie. I don't know why he would even say that. I promise you, it's not true."

"So, this is why everybody has been acting strange? This is why everybody has been bullshittin me?"

Ashley couldn't stop herself from crying. The tears just kept rolling down her face.

"Clarence, please calm down. I'm telling you the truth. I've never slept with Jason, and I've never wanted to." Clarence became so angry. He began to walk to the front door. Ashley chased after him still trying to get him to calm down.

"Clarence." She grabbed his shoulder, but he pulled away.

"Don't fuckin touch me" He opened the door but before he walked out he turned and asked her. "So, that baby in your stomach?"

"What do you mean, Clarence?" He walked outside and left the door wide open.

"Is it mine?"

"How could you ask me something like that, Clarence?"

Clarence stood in front of the door and stared her in her eyes.
Tears began to roll down her cheeks. He turned and began to walk away.

"CLARENCE!" Ashley yelled.

He stopped but didn't turn around.

"Clarence, don't leave like this. Will you just talk to me, please?"

He took a deep breath and then turned to face her. Ashley stood
there crying her eyes out. He began to walk towards her which made her
even more nervous. Not knowing what he had on his mind. Once he was
standing face to face with her, she couldn't even look him in his eyes. She
felt so ashamed. Clarence grabbed her cheeks and lifted her head until
she was looking him in his eyes. Her hands were shivering. He then
kissed her forehead and whispered into her ear.

"I believed in you."

Those were his only words. He turned again and walked off.
Ashley stood there and watched him walk away. The tears began to come
even quicker after hearing what he had to say. She had to run in the house
because she couldn't take it. She began to bawl, and she didn't want the
neighbors to hear her. She ran straight to her bedroom and laid down. She
grabbed her phone. First, she thought to call Clarence, but she figured he
wouldn't answer. She didn't even know what to say to him. So she called
Brittany. The phone rang a couple times before Brittany answered.

"Hey, Ashley, what's up?" Ashley said nothing. She was still
crying, and all Brittany could hear was her sniffing.

"Ashley. Hello, what's wrong? Girl, talk to me." It took a while for her to respond.

"Brittany, I told him."

"Told who?" Ashley began to cry even more.

"What are you talking about?" Ashley let out a deep sigh.

"I told Clarence about the situation with Jason."

"Oh no, Ashley, why?"

They both waited for the other to respond

"I told you not to tell him."

Ashley hung up the phone. She didn't want to be criticized for doing what she felt was right. Brittany called back, but she just sat and watched the phone ring. She called a few times and even sent a few text messages. Ashley just stared at the phone and watched it light up. Meanwhile, Clarence began to drive home, but his mind was racing back and forth. It seemed as if everything began to unfold. Jason wanting to move away. Ashley behaving the way she did. All those thoughts were just running through his mind. He couldn't go home.

15

Clarence needed to clear his mind, and he knew exactly where to do it. He made a U-turn and headed to Mr. Richs bar. When he pulled up, he noticed the parking lot was a little more packed than normal. He paid it no mind, parked his car, and walked inside. When he walked in, there was loud music playing and a group of women standing in a circle singing. It couldn't have been a live band because they all sounded like a pack of stray cats. Clarence walked to the bar and was immediately spotted by Mr. Rich.

"Hey there, Clarence, what's going on, son?" He reached over the bar and slapped Clarence on the back.

"Choose your poison, son, drinks are on me." This was a complete shock to Clarence. Mr. Rich wasn't known to offer free drinks.

"Just give me a Crown Royal on the rocks" Mr. Rich turned and made the drink within seconds. Almost like he knew what Clarence was going to order.

"What's going on with those women up there singing?"

"Oh, I'm starting to have karaoke nights."

Clarence turned to face the women who were all taking turns singing on one microphone. All of them were fully intoxicated. He then turned back to face Mr. Rich after he downed his first drink.

"Give me another one."

Mr. Rich had it waiting for him. He could tell something was bothering Clarence. Clarence wasn't flashing his big smile. He took down his second drink and told Mr. Rich to fix him another.

"Umm, you sure you need another, son, you're not much of a drinker." Clarence nodded his head. So, without asking again, Mr. Rich slid him another drink.

"No more after that, I see your eyes crossing, and I ain't got no time to be taking you home. I got me a piece of p"…"

Clarence slammed his glass on the bar before Mr. Rich could finish, and he walked out without saying anything. The alcohol was beginning to hit him, but he was trying to shake it off. He jumped in his car and drove out of the parking lot. Instead of driving home, he headed to Ashley's apartment. He found himself a parking spot. Clarence thought about calling her to let her know he was there, but the liquor made him change is mind. He took a deep breath before he got out of the car. While walking up the stairs, he could hear voices coming from Ashley's floor. He tried to look between the steps to see if he could see who it was. As he got closer, the voices began to sound more familiar to him. When he finally reached her floor he saw Ashley hugging. Clarence couldn't believe his eyes. It was around two in the morning, and there was a man hugging the woman who was carrying his child. He was so heartbroken. The liquor had worn off, and he was in complete shock. The man who was hugging Ashley backed away from her and watched her as she walked inside and closed the door. He turned and began to head in Clarence's direction. Clarence didn't want to be seen, so he hurried and ran down the steps. He made his way back to his car before the man had reached the last floor. Clarence jumped in his car, but he didn't start it up. He watched as the man walked to his car and waited for him to pull off. Clarence sat in his car, debating on whether he should go and speak with Ashley. He picked up his phone to call her, but for some reason he just couldn't find the nerve to dial her number. Clarence sat in the car contemplating for about a half hour. After about a half hour his phone vibrated. It was a text message from Ashley.

"Clarence, I know that you're upset, and you probably never want to see or speak to me, and I can understand, but I need you right now."

He dropped the phone in his lap before he even finished reading it. His phone vibrated again. There were more messages from Ashley. So, he began to read the rest.

"I'm pregnant with your child, Clarence. I know that things seem really crazy right now, but I need for you to trust me. I would never do anything to hurt you."

A tear dropped from his eye. This was a very tough situation for him to deal with. There were so many negative thoughts going through his mind. He was feeling like there was nobody he could trust. Not his best friend Jason. Not Ashley. He didn't read the whole message, but he scrolled down to the end of the long text to see her say.

"I love you."

After he read that, he started up his car and left the parking lot. He drove all the way home in silence. He made it home in about forty five minutes or so. When he walked inside, he pulled is phone out of his pocket and decided to text Ashley back.

"I love you more."

That was it. He couldn't find any other words to say, and he didn't want to start an argument without actually knowing what was going on. He left his phone on the sofa in the living room and went into his room and fell asleep. Ashley slept with the phone on her chest because she was anticipating a phone call from Clarence or even a text message. She began to doze off, but when her phone vibrated, it made her jump and look to see. She saw that it was a text from Clarence, and it made her relax just a little. She smiled and called him. The phone kept ringing, and then it went to voicemail. It wasn't like Clarence to not answer, so she called him again twice. But there was no answer. She began to worry, but little did she know, Clarence was not by his phone, and he was sleeping. The next morning, Clarence woke up and went into the living room to grab his phone. His phone was dead, so he went and put it on the charger. When he powered it on, there were five voicemails and ten text messages. He didn't check them right away because he knew they were probably from Ashley, and she was probably trying to apologize. So, he put the phone on his bed and began to walk into the bathroom, but before he could get away the phone began to ring. This time it wasn't Ashley, it was from a number he didn't recognize. First, he thought it was Ashley calling from another number, but he chose to answer it anyway.

"Hello?"

"Clarence, where are you? We've been trying to call you all night and all morning."

He pulled the phone away from his ear, so he could look at the number again. "

Who is this?" He asked the unfamiliar voice on the other end.

"THIS IS BRITTANY, CLARENCE, NOW WHERE ARE YOU? ASHLEY WAS IN A CAR WRECK! YOU NEED TO GET DOWN HERE TO THE HOSPITAL NOW!"

He dropped his phone in shock. His mind began to race again. Maybe he should have stayed at her apartment and talked to her. He picked the phone off the floor.

"Which hospital are you guys at?"

"We're at Cedar Creek, room one fifteen. Hurry, Clarence!"

She hung up the phone, and Clarence grabbed his keys and ran to his car. He jumped in the car, but before he started the engine, he began to look at his text messages. All of them from Ashley. They read:

"Clarence, where are you?"

"Clarence, I really want to see you I just want you to hold me all night"

"Are you home, Clarence? I want to come see you."

"I'm on my way to come and see you, please answer the phone."

"I'll be there in fifteen minutes, Clarence."

"I love you."

16

The doctors made Brittany wait in the waiting room as they ran tests on Ashley. She was trying to remain calm while she sat and fiddled with her cell phone. She sat and watched as the doctor's walked by. Some of them were leaving for the night, some of them getting ready to start their night. Some of them were going to the cafeteria. She jumped up as soon as she saw the doctor who had been in the room with Ashley.

"Hello, my name is Doctor Killborn." He held out his hand to shake while wearing a crooked grin. Brittany hesitated, but then she shook his hand.

"Doctor, how is my friend? How is her baby?" Brittany asked trying not to cry.

"Well, they are both doing ok. We still have to run a few tests on her, but they will both be just fine." He pulled out a note pad.

"Where is a Mr. Clarence? Is he here? I'd like to speak with him."

"I'm not sure where he is right now, but he should be on his way."

"Ok, well I'm going to go and check on Ashley, and hopefully by the time I return, he'll be here."

He turned to walk away, and then Brittany called out to him,

"Doctor Killborn, when will I be able to go in and talk to her?"

"Soon."

Then, he turned and walked through the same double doors that all the other doctors had come in and out of. Brittany went back to the chair she had been sitting in and picked up a magazine.

"How's she doing?"

A voice called out from behind her. When she turned around to see who it was she saw a man holding flowers which just so happened to be covering his face. She expected it to be Clarence but it wasn't. The man pulled the flowers from his face.

"Well, how is she, Brittany?" It was Jason.

"Well, the doctor said that she'd be ok, but what are you doing here? And why did you bring flowers, there is no funeral."

He chuckled and cracked a smile.

"Well, there might be one if Clarence comes in and he see you in here."

His smile quickly went away.

"Wait a minute, what is that supposed to mean?"

Brittany rolled her eyes at Jason and went back to her seat.

"Brittany, what do you mean by that?"

Jason was unaware that Ashley had already filled her in on what was going on. He had no idea that Clarence knew about him and Ashley supposedly being intimate with each other.

"Don't even worry about it, Jason, but like I asked, what exactly are you doing here?"

"You sent me a text message telling me what happened. I figured I'd come and show my support. I mean we are all friends."

She sucked her teeth and rolled her eyes once again.

"Friends don't sleep with each other, Jason, and friends don't sleep with other friends' girlfriends. So, what exactly are you doing here?"

"Brittany, I just..."

He was cut off as Doctor Killborn came through the double doors.

"Hello, Mr. Clarence. I'm Mr. Killborn."

Jason looked at Brittany and then looked back at the doctor.

"Umm, sir. I'm not Clarence, I'm his best friend."

That caused Brittany to stand to her feet.

"Sir, this is Jason, he's just an associate; calling him a friend would be doing way too much."

The doctor stood with the same confused look on his face.

"Geesh, Clarence still hasn't made it yet? Are you sure he's coming? I mean, Ashley told me that he's upset with her, but I'd think that he'd at least want to."

Brittany's phone began to ring. She ran to the chair and picked it up. It just so happened to be Clarence.

"Hello, Clarence, where the hell are you?"

"Brittany, I'm on the way. I must've ran over a nail or something because when I went outside, my tire was on flat. But I'll be there in about five minutes."

He hung up the phone before Britany could get another word in.

"Well, Brittany, your friend is awake and very alert. Would you like to go in to see her?"

Brittany walked towards the doctor.

"Of course." They both began to walk towards the double doors.

"I guess I'll just wait out here!"

Jason yelled out. Trying to make sure the two of them hadn't forgotten about him. They turned to him and nodded their heads then disappeared through the doors. The doctor walked into the room first with Brittany right on his back. Ashley's eyes were closed, but they opened when she heard them enter the room.

"Oh. My. God. Ashley, are you ok?"

Brittany wasn't a very emotional person, but to see her friend laying in a hospital bed, it really got to her. She began to cry as she got closer to the bed.

"Yes, Brittany, I'm fine. Don't cry." Brittany walked up to her and gave her a hug.

"I'm going to leave the two of you alone. I'll be back to check on you, ma'am. If you need anything, just buzz the nurse, and she'll get whatever you need."

Ashley smiled and nodded her head. He left the room. Brittany pulled a chair closer to the bed.

"Ashley, what happened?" Ashley sat up in the bed while grimacing because of the pain she felt in her back.

"Well, I was on my way to see Clarence, and all I can remember is I was texting him, and when I looked up, I ran up a curb, and I tried to get control of the car. But it flipped a couple times. After that, I can't remember anything." Brittany's eyes were full of tears.

"Oh, my goodness, Ashley, I'm just so glad you're ok. Don't ever scare me like this again. I almost had a heart attack." Ashley smiled.

"I'm sorry, Brittany, I just hope Clarence doesn't hate me."

"He's on his way, Ashley; I called him and told him." That brought another smile to Ashley's face.

"Listen, Brittany, I'm sorry about all of this confusion between all of us, but I promise you, I've never done..." Ashley stopped because Brittany began shaking her head.

"This isn't the time to talk about that, girl. Plus, I'm over it. I'm just glad my friend is ok. No matter what, I'll always love you." She stood and leaned in to hug her friend.

Meanwhile in the waiting room Clarence came bursting through the doors. He ran to the receptionist to let them know who he was looking for. The nurse picked up the phone to page doctor Killborn.

"Doctor Killborn, you're needed at the front desk. Doctor Killborn, you're needed at the front desk."

"Thank you so much,"

Clarence told the receptionist. He then turned and began to walk towards an empty seat, and then he saw Jason coming out of the restroom. They both stared each other down. Clarence began shaking his head. The doctor came walking through the doors holding a clipboard in his hand.

"Hello, Clarence," he called out. Clarence didn't turn around though. His attention was stuck on Jason, and he slowly began to take his jacket off. The doctor noticed there was tension, so he walked over and stood in front of Clarence.

"Clarence, why don't you come with me, Ashley has been waiting for you." Hearing Ashley's name calmed him down for a few seconds.

"Come on, son."

The doctor headed towards the double doors. Clarence began to follow him, but before he made it to the door, he turned back to face Jason. The doctor kept walking because he thought Clarence was right behind him. Clarence slowly began walking towards Jason. The nurse picked up her phone and dialed security because she had no idea what was about to happen. After a few steps, Clarence and Jason were both standing face to face.

17

Things began to get heated in the lobby between Clarence and Jason. It didn't take security long to come in and break things up. Meanwhile, Ashley and Brittany were still holding each other's hand in Ashley's room.

"I know this isn't the place to talk about things between me and Jason, but Brittany, I have to."

Brittany shook her head.

"Listen, Brittany just give me a chance to explain things to you" Brittany let go of her hand.

"Me and Jason never had anything major happen between us. We went out twice, and it was the worst experience I've ever had." Again, Brittany just shook her head.

"Well, I know exactly what you mean, Ashley." Ashley paused before she spoke again.

"What do you mean? I thought you liked Jason." Brittany laughed at her assumption.

"No, I can't stand that man; he's very egotistical, and I can't stand that."

"So, why did you deal with him for as long as you did?" Again, Brittany couldn't do anything but laugh.

"The sex is good. I mean, that's all it's been between us." This caused Ashley to shake her head.

"Brittany, why do you keep settling for these jerks? I mean, why do you even give them piece of yourself?" Brittany stood up from her seat.

"You're a beautiful woman who actually has more to offer than just a piece of your body, but you have to realize that."

Brittany seemed to be uncomfortable with where the conversation was heading. She was never really good with expressing herself. Tears began to fall down her face. "What's wrong, Brittany" Ashley held out her hand trying to get Brittany to come back closer to the bed.

"You think I like settling, Ashley? I mean, these men don't love me. They make me feel like they're so into me when all they want is sex, and I always fall for it. I hate that I can be so weak minded."

Ashley closed her eyes and shook her head. She was the one in pain physically, but her friend's pain seemed more mental.

"I mean, I know it sounds crazy, but it's like I feel so close to a man when we're having sex. Whether it's for thirty minutes or three hours, I feel like he actually cares for me, and he'll never leave me." She walked back to the chair she had pulled to the bed and sat down.

"The sex is like my drug; it takes me away from all the pain I hold inside, and when it's all over, I'm back to reality, and I feel so alone. But I never like to show it because I don't want people thinking I'm crazy or whatever." She tried to laugh it off.

"I'm jealous of you, Ashley." This caught Ashley off guard.

"Why exactly would you be jealous of me, Brittany?"

"Because you have a man who actually cares about you and who stands by you. Clarence is a good man, and you're lucky to have him." That statement seemed to hit Ashley pretty hard because her eyes began to water.

"I feel like I'm losing him; it's been so much drama, and I know no matter how good of a man he is, no man wants to put up with a bunch of nonsense, especially when it involves another man."

"Ashley, what exactly happened that night between you and Jason? Tell me the truth." She grabbed Ashley's hand.

"Nothing happened, I asked him to come over and fix my shower and he did. There was nothing more than that." They stared each other in the eyes.

"He tried to make a move on me, but I put him out. Brittany, you know I'm not like that; I would never do Clarence like that."

"Well, why would Jason even say anything like that? I mean, what exactly is he trying to do?" Brittany's phone began to ring, but she ignored it.

"I don't know, Brittany. I really don't know."

Back in the lobby, the security escorted Jason outside, and Doctor Killborn came back to get Clarence, so he could take him to see Ashley. Clarence walked into the room behind the doctor to see Brittany and Ashley giving each other a hug.

"Well, isn't this a lovely scene!" The doctor yelled out which caused the two of them to break into laughter.

"Ashley, I have someone here to see you." Clarence came from behind the doctor and walked up to the bed.

"Doctor Killborn, can you show me where the cafeteria is, I'm starving." Brittany stood up and walked towards him. She turned back to speak to Ashley before leaving.

"Ashley, I'll be back." She hit Clarence on his shoulder as she walked past him while saying,

"Bout time you made it." She smiled at him to assure him that she wasn't being too serious. The doctor and Brittany left the room. Clarence walked to the bed and sat in the seat that Brittany had been using. He didn't hug or kiss Ashley. He just sat there and stared at her.

"Clarence what's wrong? Why are you looking at me like that?" It took him a while to speak as he gathered his thoughts. Clarence took a deep breath.

"I love you more than you'll ever know, but I just can't do this anymore."

18

"What do you mean you can't do this anymore, Clarence?" Ashley leaned closer to him.

"What does that mean, talk to me, please?" Again, tears began to fall down her face.

"This is just too much for me, Ashley, all the lies, the secrets, the drama; that's not what I need in my life." He stood to his feet and pushed the chair back.

"I'm just tired of waking up not knowing what's going on between us and having so many mixed emotions. One minute, I'm happy and thinking about our future, and the next, I'm sad, wondering if there's even a future for us. It makes me wonder if you even care about me."

"Of course, I care, Clarence. You know I do." He just looked at her and shook his head.

"If you care, why would you keep so much from me? I mean, what exactly are we doing here?"

"What do you mean what are we doing?" She tried to get up from the bed, but the pain in her back wouldn't allow it.

"You know what, Ashley, don't even worry about it."

"Clarence, don't do this; talk to me. How can we get through this if you won't open up to me?" He began to walk towards the door.

"Clarence, what about the baby?" He stopped walking and stood still.

"Did you forget that I'm pregnant with your child?" That statement struck a nerve with him and he turned back and walked back to the bed.

"You want to talk, Ashley? Ok, let's talk." Clarence tried his best not to yell and be too aggressive because he didn't want to scare Ashley.

"Let's talk about how Jason thinks the baby is his. I mean, what would make him think that?"

"Clarence, I don't know. I really don't know why he would even say something like that. I wish I never even went out with him. This has caused me so much stress. I would never do that to you." She watched as Clarence just stood there with anger all in his face shaking his head.

"That's bullshit, I mean there has to be some reason, but I guess that's just something else you're keeping from me."

"Clarence, I never slept with him. Maybe you should ask him yourself why he caused all this nonsense." She could tell that Clarence was close to losing his cool. "Clarence, please calm down. I'm sorry that things have turned out this way. I mean, do you think I want things to be like this? I'm pregnant. This isn't healthy; I'm laying here in a hospital bed. If you leave me, I'll be all alone, I don't have anybody else; I need you."

"What about John?" That caught her by surprise.

"What about John? Why would you even bring his name up?" Clarence walked to the other side of the bed.

"Oh so, now you're just going to act clueless?"

"Clarence, what are you talking about?" He put his hands on his face and let out a slight moan.

"I saw him at your apartment. I saw the two of you hugging. What was he doing at your apartment that late?"

"Oh my, God, Clarence. Really?"

He waited for her to explain.

"He came by to talk to me about this situation with you I needed advice and he gave it to me"

"WHAT THE HELL DO YOU NEED ADVICE FROM HIM FOR"

He began to raise his voice and it made Ashley uncomfortable.

"I asked him what should I do with this situation between you and he told me I should tell you the truth and try and fix things between us because we're having a child together he's just my friend and he was very supportive when I needed him to be I mean I didn't know what to do Clarence I'm sorry I know I should've came to you and talked to you about everything but I didn't know how you would take it"

As she finished her sentence, Doctor Kilburn walked back into the room.

"He you guys is everything ok?"

They both looked at him, and neither responded right away.

"Yeah doc everything is just fine can you give us a few more minutes please" The doctor nodded his head.

"Yes of course but Ashley we have to run a few more x-rays so I'll be back in a few"

She nodded her head in return. Doctor Kilburn left the room again.

"I just don't understand you Ashley you say you love me but you talk to everybody but me and I'm the first person you should come to I feel like I can't trust you"

Ashley fought her way out of the bed. She walked up to Clarence.

"Clarence, listen to me, I'm telling you the truth. Right now, you're just upset there's a lot going on at once, and I understand your frustration with me, but I'm willing to do whatever it takes to regain your trust, just give me a chance." She placed both her hands on his face.

"Clarence just give me a chance please if you leave what am I going to do am I supposed to go to the doctor appointments alone what about when the baby gets here, will you even be around?"

For the moment, he didn't have any words. He just mumbled. "I can't believe this is happening."

Ashley took a deep breath.

"I love you, Clarence, and I promise I'll never keep anything from you again."

They both locked eyes. Both of their eyes were filled with tears.

"I wish you would've made that decision sooner."

He kissed her forehead and moved her hands from his face.

"What does that mean, Clarence?"

He walked to the door. Before he walked out, he turned to look at her once again, but he didn't say a word.

"CLARENCE!"

Ashley yelled out his name as he walked out of the room. That caused her to break down completely. She had no idea what his words

125

meant. She didn't know if he was saying goodbye or if he just needed time alone but there she was all alone once again. Brittany came back into the room shortly after Clarence left.

"I'm definitely never eating in that cafeteria again."

She didn't notice her friend was in tears as she made her way back to her chair.

"They had me waiting all that time, and then my food was cold, it was cold, Ashley. You know I don't like no cold."

She stopped when she heard Ashley sniffing behind her.

"What's wrong, Ashley?"

Ashley began crying even harder. Her body began to shake.

"Ashley, did Clarence do something to you?"

It was so hard for her to speak. The tears just kept rolling as she cried like a helpless child. Brittany stood from the chair and wrapped her arms around Ashley.

"He's gone, Brittany."

"What do you mean he's gone?"

Brittany leaned back so she could look Ashley in her eyes.

"He told me he couldn't do it anymore, I think I've lost him for good."

"Wait a minute; he does remember that you're pregnant right?"

That wasn't the best question to ask because it made her cry even more.

"I'm sorry, Ashley. Look, let him leave, if he doesn't want to be around, oh well. Screw him. I'm going to be here for you and the baby."

They hugged again.

"I know you will, Brittany, but I didn't want to go through this. I didn't think he would leave; it's like he doesn't care anymore, and I understand why. I've put him through too much."

She grabbed the box of Kleenex that was sitting next to her bed and blew her nose.

"I understand what you're saying, Ashley, but you told him the truth. If he didn't want to accept it, there's nothing more you can do."

Ashley was at a loss for words. All she could do was shake her head. The night ended, and both Brittany and Ashley had fallen asleep. They were both awakened to a nurse coming into the room to check on Ashley.

"Good morning, ladies, rise and shine"

They both began to stretch, and Brittany let out a loud moan.

"My neck is killing me. I can't believe I fell asleep in this chair."

She stood up and tried to move her neck, but the pain she felt from sleeping so awkwardly wouldn't allow her to.

"Well, ma'am, we have good news for you."

Ashley turned her attention from Brittany to the nurse.

"Yes, nurse, what is it?"

The nurse walked over to her bed and placed her hand on Ashley's shoulder.

"Well, you and the baby are just fine; you have no fractures or any structural damage, so you guys can go home today."

"But nurse, I have these pains in my back" The doctor nodded her head.

"Oh that's common when a person is in a car wreck; we'll get you some pain meds, and it shouldn't last long—maybe a few days."

She walked to the end of the bed to grab the clipboard that was placed there by Doctor Kilburn.

"I'm going to go and get your paper work, and Doctor Kilburn should be in, and he'll come and speak with you. And then, you're good to go."

Ashley smiled at the nurse, and then she turned and walked out of the room.

"Thank, God, Ashley. I'm glad the baby is ok."

"Yes, me too." Brittany walked to the front of the bed.

"Well, I'm going to go and get some coffee; do you want some?"

"No. I'm ok; I'm just ready to go."

Brittany hurried and left the room. In walked Doctor Kilburn. He spoke with Ashley for a few minutes and gave her a prescription for the pain medicine. Brittany drove Ashley home and helped her get settled in before she headed to her own apartment to get some rest. Weeks went by and everyday Brittany would stop by and check on Ashley. Most of the time she spend the night with her. She would drive Ashley to her doctor appointments. It almost seemed like they were roommates. After about two months or so they had their own little routine set up. The whole two months Ashley heard nothing from Clarence. No calls or text. NOTHING. Then, one night at Ashley's apartment, Brittany came storming in. She had been there so much, Ashley had her a key made, so she wouldn't always have to get up and open the door. When she came in, the look on her face scared Ashley.

"Brittany, what's wrong?"

Brittany walked into the kitchen grabbed herself a glass and filled it with wine that had been sitting in the fridge. She walked into the living room and sat on the sofa. Her facial expression hadn't changed.

"Ashley, please come and sit next to me." Ashley walked into the living room and sat next to her. She held out her hand.

"Hold my hand, Ashley."

"Brittany what is going on? You're scaring me." She grabbed Brittany's hand and noticed a tear drop from her cheek.

"Ashley, he's dead."

"Wait a minute, Brittany, who are you talking about?"

Ashley asked as she watched her friend rock back and forth on the sofa. Her hands were shaking and tears began to roll down her face.

"Brittany, please."

Ashley already hormonal because of the baby began to cry.

"Ashley, I can't believe this is happening."

She stood up and walked into the kitchen to re-fill her glass. She didn't wait to get into the living room to drink it; she hurried and drank it then poured some more. Ashley stood to her feet and walked into the kitchen. She took the wine bottle and glass from Brittany and sat it on the counter. Ashley then grabbed Brittany by the shoulders.

"Now, tell me what is going on; calm down and talk to me." Brittany tried to gather herself.

"Tell me who is dead."

"JASON!"

Her response made Ashley's heart drop. Not because she was saddened by the news, but because she was more relieved that it wasn't who she thought it was. It also brought some confusion to her. Brittany had been saying how much she couldn't stand Jason and wished she never met him.

"Oh my, God. Brittany, no, what happened?"

She tried to be sympathetic, but it sounded more like sarcasm.

"I don't know, Ashley, someone killed him." Ashley tried to hide the confused look on her face.

"How do you know this? I thought you cut off all communication with him."

Brittany tried to grab for the wine glass, but Ashley grabbed her arm and shook her head no.

"I did, but apparently the police found my number in his phone, and they called me and asked me a whole bunch of questions. I even went to identify his body because they couldn't get in touch with any of his family members."

"WOW, this is crazy. I can't believe this don't take this the wrong way, Brittany, but I thought you said you wished that he would just go away and die why are you crying so hard?"

Brittany looked at Ashley and showed her frustration with question.

"I didn't mean that literally, Ashley. I just wanted him to go away; I didn't actually want him to die."

They both walked into the living room and sat back on the sofa.

"I wonder if Clarence knows anything."

Ashley said. She said it out loud but actually was speaking to herself. Hoping that it had nothing to do with Clarence. She hadn't heard from Clarence since he left her alone at the hospital.

"I'm sure he has. I mean, they were best friends"

"They were," Ashley snapped at Brittany.

"Well, call him, Ashley. I'm sure he's hurting. I mean, no matter how bad things were between them they were like brothers, and I'm sure he needs your comfort."

Ashley hesitated before she responded. She thought about calling him, but at the moment, couldn't build up the courage. She missed him, and she wanted to be there for him.

"What are you waiting for?"

Ashley jumped up and went to the bedroom to grab her phone. She walked into the bathroom and closed the door. She needed to gather her thoughts before she called him. She didn't go back into the living room with Brittany because she didn't want her all in the conversation. The phone rang a couple times, and then Clarence picked up.

"Hello?"

Ashley didn't respond right away. She was nervous and didn't know what to say.

"HELLO!" Clarence yelled out on the other end of the phone.

"Clarence, are you ok?"

"Who is this?" That caught Ashley off guard. She wasn't expecting Clarence to not recognize her voice.

"Umm, hello who is this?" He asked again.

"Ashley!" she yelled out just before he hung up the phone.

131

"Clarence, why don't you have my number in your phone?"

"Is there something that you need, Ashley? I have a lot going on right now."

Ashley was in complete shock. Though she and Clarence hadn't spoken in a couple months, she couldn't believe how cold he was being to her. "Yes, Clarence, I just wanted to see if you were..." "I'll talk to you later." he cut her off and before she could respond he hung up the phone. "Hello?"

"Clarence."

She looked at her phone and the screen read "Call ended" She walked out the bathroom and back into the living room. Brittany was still sitting on the sofa with her face in one of the pillows. She felt Ashley sit down on the sofa so she lifted her head up.

"Did you talk to him?" Ashley nodded her head.

"Well, what did he say, does he know anything, did he tell you what happened?"

Ashley just shook her head while staring at the wall. Trying her best to hold back the tears.

"ASHLEY, I NEED TO KNOW WHAT HAPPENED TO JASON!"

Brittany began to yell. She was hurting, and she wanted to know what was going on.

"He didn't even know who I was, Brittany, and he hung up in my face."

She stood up and walked back into her bedroom. When she came back into the living room, she had on her jacket and then she walked into the kitchen to grab her purse.

"Give me your keys, Brittany." She held out her hand.

"Where are you going, Ashley?" Brittany jumped from the sofa.

"I need to go talk to him face to face"

"No, ma'am, you are not going without me. I'm driving you" Ashley walked to the door and turned around.

"Well, come on, let's go."

Brittany grabbed her purse, and they both walked out of the apartment. The sky was very dark and there was a slight drizzle. Ashley directed Brittany on how to get to Clarence apartment. When they arrived, they immediately found a parking spot. The rain had picked up when they were on their way, but once they made it to his apartment, it suddenly stopped.

"Just wait here for me, Brittany. I'll be back."

She grabbed Ashley's arm before she could get out.

"Are you sure you don't need me to go with you?"

Ashley snatched her arm away and climbed out of the car. Brittany rolled her window down and yelled out "At least call him first."

Ashley didn't pay her any mind and walked to his apartment without calling. Once she made it to his door, she held out her arm to knock on the door but before she could the door opened and a woman walked out. A woman she had never seen before. Her mouth dropped, and Clarence came walking after the woman.

"Goodbye Clarence"

133

The woman waved to him as she headed for the parking lot. Clarence turned his attention to Ashley and stared her down. The look on his face was a look Ashley wasn't used to seeing. He just stood in front of her seeming so emotionless.

He then asked her, "What are you doing here?"

19

Ashley stood in silence for a few seconds before Clarence asked her again.

"Ashley, why are you here?"

Ashley pushed Clarence out the way and walked into his apartment. He shook his head then closed the door.

"Clarence, who was that woman?"

Clarence sucked his teeth and just shook his head.

"CLARENCE!"

Ashley walked up to him and stood in his face. He couldn't even look her in the face. It was almost like he had something to hide.

"Is that why I haven't heard from you?" Clarence still had no words for her.

"HELLO, CLARENCE!" Her voice began to get louder as she became even angrier.

"No wonder I haven't heard from you; you've been hiding from me with whoever that woman was."

Clarence looked her in her eyes and noticed that she began to cry.

"You left me in a hospital by myself, and I'm pregnant with your child. How could you do me?

"HOW DO I EVEN KNOW IF THAT'S MY CHILD OR NOT?"

Ashley's mouth dropped.

"How can you even ask me something like that, Clarence?"

"Because you slept with Ja."

"Don't you dare say that to me, Clarence. You're a grown ass man, and you're still doing that he say she say bullshit." Clarence walked to the door and opened it.

"Look, Ashley, I don't have time to argue with you about this. I'm dealing with a lot right now, and this arguing isn't going to make things worse."

"I suggest you close the door, Clarence, because I'm not leaving; we're going to talk. I'm tired of this walking out shit. I'm tired of wondering what's going on in your head, so close that door and talk to me."

He looked at her and saw the serious look on her face and immediately closed the door. Ashley made her way into the living room and waited for him to follow. Clarence walked into the living room but didn't sit down right away.

"Clarence, come sit next to me."

Clarence let out a sigh and made his way to the sofa where Ashley was sitting. He plopped down on the sofa. Still not looking at Ashley. They both sat in silence for a few minutes. Both trying to gather their thoughts.

"Her name is Melinda." Ashley turned her whole body on the sofa, so that she was facing Clarence completely. Clarence sat staring at the wall.

"Well, who is this Melinda woman, Clarence?" Ashley tried her best not to cry, but of course, that was impossible.

"She's a bartender, Ashley."

"Well are you sleeping with this woman?"

The question seemed to bother Clarence. He turned to face Ashley.

"No, Ashley she's been here trying to console me."

Ashley didn't know what to believe. She didn't want to argue with him because he just lost his best friend. Even though Clarence and Jason had been going through a tough time, she knew how close they were. Damn near brothers.

"What happened to Jason?" Clarence began to shake his head.

"Clarence did you." She paused when she saw the look Clarence gave her.

"Ashley, I don't know what happened to him."

Ashley noticed that Clarence was beginning to feel uneasy, so she moved closer to him. She grabbed his hand as he began to tell his side of the story.

"When, I left you at the hospital, I went to the bar to talk to Mr. Rich, and Jason was there; he tried to talk to me, but I didn't want to hear anything he had to say."

A tear dropped from his face.

"I admit, I wanted to hurt him bad the only thing stopped me was the thought of never being able to hold you again."

Those words caught Ashley by surprise.

"Are you serious, Clarence? You haven't called or anything in so long; do you know how hard it is for me to believe that?"

"I know I messed up, Ashley, but have you ever thought about how I was feeling?"

He tried to stand up, but she grabbed his arm and pulled him back down.

"Every day, Clarence, but you can't just walk out on me like that. I mean, did you even think about me and the baby?"

"Of course I did, Ashley, but I was upset. I'm not saying what I've done is acceptable, and I'm sorry I even behaved that way; it's not the kind of man I want to be."

They both began to get a better feel for each other which helped lighten the mood.

"So, what happened after you told him you didn't want to hear what he had to say?"

"I don't even know."

She began to squeeze his hand. In her mind, she was expecting the worst. She began to wonder what if Clarence was the cause for Jason's demise.

"All I remember is he had a couple drinks and then left the bar, that's all I know."

"Are you sure, Clarence?" Again, he gave her that look which made her look in another direction.

"Ashley, I'm telling you the truth. I've told the police the truth."

He pulled his hand from hers and stood to his feet.

"I never expected anything like this to happen, Ashley. I wish I would've at least heard him out, but I was too stubborn and now he's gone."

"Clarence, you can't beat yourself up about it; eventually the truth will come out. I know he was your best friend, and I know it hurts, but what about me and your baby? We need you."

She stood and walked up to Clarence.

"I'm sorry, Ashley. I really am. I promise I'll never leave the two of you again, but you have to promise that you'll never keep any secrets from me."

She wrapped her arms around him and looked up into his eyes.

"I promise, Clarence, no more secrets."

They hugged each other. After a few seconds, Ashley pulled back

"Ouch!" she yelled out.

"What? What did I do?"

"Nothing, Clarence. I think it's just heartburn."

He put his arm around her as she began to rub her chest. They stood next to each other until they heard someone knocking on the door.

"Let me see who that is, Ashley."

Ashley continued to rub on her chest. The heartburn had begun to hit her even harder.

"Ok, I'm going to get me a glass of water." She walked into the kitchen as Clarence went to answer the door. He looked through the peep hole before he opened it. When he noticed who it was, he put his head against the door.

"Oh God," he mumbled to himself. Then, he cracked the door.

"Clarence, where is Ashley?"

It was Brittany on the other side of the door.

"And why are you cracking the door like you don't know me?"

Clarence opened the door and let her in. Ashley came from the kitchen and began to walk towards Brittany and Clarence.

"Oh my, God, Brittany. I'm so sorry for making you wait for so long."

"You could have at least called my phone to check on me, Ashley."

She quickly turned her attention back to Clarence.

"Clarence, how are you holding up?"

Clarence tried not to make eye contact with Brittany because he didn't want her to see the emotion in his face.

"I'm dealing with it."

"What does that mean, Clarence?" He looked at Ashley as Brittany tried to get his attention.

"I don't know what to say, Brittany. I mean, it's hard to deal with. Jason was like my brother, and now he's no longer here. I just hate the fact that we never had the chance to sit down and talk about things that were going on, so now I'm left with a lot of confusion."

Brittany just stared at him while he talked.

"So, do you know what happened to him? I mean, have you heard anything?"

Again, he looked at Ashley. Ashley stared back at him and waited for his response.

"I saw him after I left the hospital; he tried to speak to me, but I didn't want to hear anything he had to say"

Clarence told his side of the story yet again only this time he seemed more emotional. Brittany made him feel as if she was interrogating him. She stared him down like she felt like he was the one who murdered Jason. She just wanted answers. She just didn't want to hurt Ashley, so she had to watch how she approached him.

"I feel the same way, Clarence. I wish I could have sat down and talked to him about everything. I mean, there was just so much confusion, and now I'm stuck with so many unanswered questions."

Clarence just stared at the floor and shook his head.

"Well, I have to run a few errands. Ashley, are you ready to go?" Ashley looked surprised.

"Umm, yeah I guess, Brittany."

"Ok, well, I'm going to go wait in the car, and, Clarence, stay strong, sir. Everything will be ok."

She walked outside and closed the door behind her. Ashley began walking towards the door but before she could make it Clarence stopped her.

"Please, don't leave me, Ashley. I don't want to be here alone." Ashley gave Clarence a hug and whispered in his ear

"Well, maybe you should call Melinda back over."

She then walked out of the apartment. Clarence was dumbfounded. He turned around to walk into his bedroom then he heard the door open. Ashley made her way back inside.

"I told Brittany she could go ahead and leave me here."

Clarence stood and tried to figure out why she came back after saying what she said.

"But I thought you..." Ashley walked to him and gave him a kiss. They continued to kiss and made their way into the bedroom. They both had so many mixed emotions they felt they needed to let out, and the way they were able to do so was to have sex. They made love like never before.

Clarence was very gentle with her body because he was afraid he may do something that would affect the baby. While he was on top of her, he took his time and moved in and out gently.

"Clarence, I need to feel all of you; don't be afraid, the baby is just fine."

Clarence hesitated at first, but then he began to go deeper until he felt Ashley reach her climax. Her orgasm felt better than ever. It felt like it was her first time being with Clarence. Afterwards, they both laid next to each other completely naked. Ashley laid her head on Clarence's' chest.

"Clarence, do you think we're going to have a boy or a girl?"

He smiled after hearing her question.

"I'm hoping we have a girl, and if we do, I know she'll be just as beautiful as her mother."

"Aww, you're so sweet, baby I wouldn't mind having a girl but what do you think we should name her?"

Clarence sighed. This time it was a sigh of relief. He felt as ease again.

"What about, Claudine?"

"Eww, Clarence, no. We will not name my baby that name."

He laughed at her disapproval.

"I don't know, sweetheart. I'll let you pick the name."

"And what if we have a boy, Clarence, don't think you're going to name him Clarence because that name is too common, and I want my child to be different."

His smile quickly turned into a frown.

"My name is not too common, and of course his name will be Clarence; he's my first son." Ashley sucked her teeth.

"Anyways, whenever we find out what we're having, we'll pick five names for each gender, and we'll pick which one's we like the most."

"Ok, baby, whatever you want to do."

He kissed her forehead and pulled her closer to him. She began to feel the pain in her chest again. Clarence felt her pull back and noticed that she was in pain.

"Are you ok, baby?"

"I'm fine, Clarence, it's just the heartburn again.

She got up from the bed and walked into the restroom. She had to grab a towel because her face was drenched in sweat. Ashley then made her way back into the bedroom and laid next to Clarence. She could tell that he was worried by the way he looked at her.

"Don't look like that, Clarence, I'm fine."

She didn't want to worry him, so she kept telling him over and over that she was fine, though the heartburn kept her up the whole night.

20

Clarence fell asleep and slept pretty much the whole night. Ashley was dealing with the pains, so she didn't get much sleep. She kept getting up and going to the restroom. Every time she got up she moved slowly because she didn't want to wake Clarence. She was finally able to fall asleep, but it seemed like just when she closed her eyes, it was already time for her to wake up. She woke up and heard Clarence in the bathroom. He poked his head into the bedroom and saw that she was awake.

"Hey, baby, do you want to go and get breakfast?"

He had to take his tooth brush out of his mouth just so she could understand me.

"Well, I have a doctor's appointment today, Clarence." He went back into the restroom to rinse out his mouth.

"Well, let me take you," he said to her as he walked back into the bed room wearing a towel around his neck.

"Ok, that's fine, but I need to go home and change first."

"That's fine, let me throw on some clothes, and we can go." He saw her rubbing on her chest again.

"Maybe you need to tell the doctor about that heartburn. I mean, I'm not used to being around a pregnant woman, but I don't think heartburn should last that long."

She looked at Clarence and rolled her eyes.

"Clarence, can you hurry and get dressed? I don't want to be late for my appointment."

He hurried and got dressed, and afterwards, they were on their way to Ashley's apartment. She went inside the apartment and went straight to the bathroom. She began to run the shower, and then her phone began to ring.

"Clarence, can you answer that, and tell them I'm in the shower."

Clarence grabbed the phone and noticed it was from an unknown number.

"Hello?" He looked at the screen to see if the person had hung up but they didn't. There just was no response on the other end.

"Hello?" Clarence called out again. Still no response, so he hung up. After taking a shower, Ashley came into the room with a towel wrapped around her body.

"Who was that on the phone, baby?" Clarence shrugged his shoulders.

"What does that mean, Clarence, who was it?"

"I don't know, baby, they didn't say anything."

His phone began to ring. He pulled the phone out of his pocket and answered it.

"Hey, I'm kind of busy right now, can I call you back?"

"Clarence, don't hang..." he hung up the phone before the person on the other end of the phone could finish. He jumped up and noticed that Ashley was giving him a look like she knew he was up to no good.

"Who was that, Clarence?"

"HUH?" She folded her arms and waited for his response.

"Nobody important, Ashley, now come on, let's go. We're going to be late."

She didn't want to start an argument, so she walked back into the bathroom to finish getting dressed.

"Clarence, you do know this is the most important doctor visit?"

She yelled out from the bathroom. Clarence walked into the bathroom.

"Oh really, why is that?" Again, she gave him that look and shook her head.

"Duh, Clarence, we find out what we're having. Do you pay attention to anything?"

To avoid saying the wrong thing, Clarence played it off as if he already knew what she was talking about.

"Oh yeah, duh. I'm so excited."

"Anyways, come on, Clarence, let's go."

They both made their way out of the apartment. While walking down the steps, Clarence felt his phone vibrate. He pulled it out, and there was a text message from the same number who had called him while he was in the room with Ashley.

"Clarence, you need to come and talk to me ASAP."

He put his phone back into his pocket. They got into the car and headed to the doctor's office. Clarence pulled into the parking lot at the doctor's office. Then, he jumped out the car and walked over to open Ashley's door and help her out. She didn't feel like getting too dressed up, so she had just thrown on a pair of sweats and tennis shoes. While walking towards the doctor's office, they saw John and his wife coming out. John spoke out.

"Hey, Ashley. Hey, Clarence, how you guy's doing and how's the baby?"

"We're fine, and we're about to go check on the baby right now." Ashley responded. John had a big smile on his face.

"Oh ok, do you guys know what y'all are having?" John's wife asked Ashley.

"That's the main thing we're here for." Ashley hugged John and then hugged his wife.

"It was nice seeing you guys, but I have to get in here. I'm already late."

"Ok, well, congrats again, Ashley."

John's wife began to walk to the parking lot. John's smile quickly faded.

"Clarence, I heard what happened to your friend, Jason. Man, that's terrible, I'm sorry to hear that."

Clarence looked on with a very nervous look on his face. As if he was being questioned by an officer or something.

"Yeah, it's tough to deal with." John reached out and patted him on the shoulder.

"Well, I have to get going, my wife is ready to eat, and you know how pregnant women have to eat or else they'll get all crazy."

He chuckled, but Clarence still had the nervous look on his face.

"See ya later, John, and good luck with the baby, man."

He walked into the parking lot to join his wife. They both got into the car and drove off. Clarence walked into the building and looked around the waiting room but didn't see Ashley. So, he walked up to the

147

secretary and asked if she had seen her. The secretary told him which room Ashley had went to. When he made his way to the room, he looked into the room and Ashley noticed him through the small window, and she waved at him to let him know it was ok to come in.

"Are you ready to find out, Clarence?"

"HUH?" Clarence responded.

"The baby, Clarence, are you ready to find out what we're having?"

"Oh yeah, baby. I told you I'm excited."

He still had the nervous look on his face. The doctor came into the room and ran the ultrasound. After running the ultrasound, the doctor left and came back with an envelope.

"Ok, you guys. I'm going to let you two open this, and on this inside, it's a card from us that'll let you know the sex of the baby." He gave the card to Ashley.

"Now, I'm going to leave the two of you alone while you look at the card." He jumped up from his stool and left the room. Clarence felt his phone vibrate again.

"Clarence, where are you?"

"Clarence, you need to get down here quick; some guys came in here looking for you, and I think they're police. They said they need to talk to you."

He put the phone back into his pocket, and he stared at the window. It was almost like he was stuck in a daze. All he could hear was Ashley calling out his name.

"CLARENCE!"

"CLARENCE!"

"CLARENCE!"

He finally snapped out of the daze.

"Clarence, what's wrong?" He shook his head.

"Nothing, baby, um, just open up the card let's see what we're having."

He walked over to her and placed his hand on her shoulder. She opened up the card and it read: "Congrats, you're having a boy!"

"So, this means we're having a Jr. Right?"

Clarence asked Ashley as she sat the card on her lap.

"We're having a boy, but I don't know about a Jr."

Her response brought a frown to his face.

"Uhh, what's wrong with him being a Jr.?"

"Clarence is a common name, sweetheart, and I want to name him something different."

As she spoke, his phone began to ring again. He picked it up without any hesitation.

"Hey, look, I'm going to come speak to you later, ok?"

Without giving the person a chance to respond he hung up the phone. Ashley didn't even look his way. She was so excited to finally find out the sex of the baby. They spent a little more time in the room before speaking with the doctor again and then they made their way back to the parking lot.

"Clarence can we go somewhere and sit down to eat."

She asked as she waited for him to open her door. As he opened her door he responded by saying

"I would love to do that, baby, but I have some business to tend to, and it's really important."

All she could do was shake her head. She tried giving him a look like a child would do when they don't get their way, but it didn't work out too well.

"Ashley, please don't be mad; it's not what you think it is. I promise you, as soon as I'm done, I'll come get you, and we can go out to eat, ok?"

"Whatever, Clarence, just take me home."

She folded her arms across her chest. The ride back to her apartment was a very quiet one. When they arrived, Clarence parked the car and leaned in for a kiss. Ashley pulled her face away.

"Ashley, what's wrong now?" She had no answer for him, so he asked again.

"Clarence, there's nothing wrong, so leave it alone."

She opened up her door and began to climb out. Clarence grabbed her arm which made her jerk away from him.

"I love you, Ashley."

She took and deep breath and mumbled, "I love you too."

And just like that, she got out of the car and walked away. Clarence didn't chase after her to try and make things right because he needed to speak with the person who had been calling his phone. He called the number back.

"Hey, meet me at Mr. Rich's bar in twenty five minutes."

"Clarence, I'm already here, so come on."

Clarence sped out of the parking lot and headed for the bar. Once he arrived, the parking lot was pretty much empty. About two cars or so. He recognized because it belonged to Mr. Rich. Clarence couldn't even park straight because he was so paranoid. So, his car was taking up two spots. He jumped out of his car and ran into the bar. There he saw Melinda sitting alone at a table waiting for him.

"Join me, Clarence." She pointed at an empty chair that was sitting in front of her.

"Melinda, what the hell is going on?"

Clarence stared into her eyes. She sensed that he was very nervous.

"Clarence, do you need me to get you a drink?" He just shook his head.

"No, I can't think about drinking right now."

"Well, Clarence, I'll be straight forward with you." She leaned on to the table.

"Word going around is that you're the one who killed Jason."

"WHAT?" Clarence yelled out. He looked around to make sure there was no one else in the bar.

"What would make people think that? I mean, that's crazy."

His hands began to tremble. Again, Melinda noticed how nervous he was. She grabbed his hands and stared him into his eyes.

"Clarence, listen to me, now is not the time to lie and run but..."

"Not you too, Melinda. I thought we were friends."

He moved his hands from underneath hers.

"Clarence, we are friends, that's why I'm trying to help you out, but you have to talk to me and tell me what happened that night or at least try and remember."

"Melinda, what do you mean try and remember?"

She dropped her head in frustration.

"Clarence, that night, you were very drunk, so you probably don't remember much."

Just as she finished her sentence, Mr. Rich made his way through the front door.

"Well, look what we have here"

He came in wearing his normal long black trench coat. If you didn't know Mr. Rich and just so happened to see him, you'd think he was a member of the mafia or some type of gang.

"Don't you two look like a married couple?" He laughed and walked up to Clarence.

"Clarence, I'm sorry to hear about you friend, son, it kills me inside because I knew him since he was a boy."

"Mr. Rich, I don't mean to interrupt, but can you excuse us? We're talking about something really important."

Mr. Rich didn't even utter a word; he just shrugged his shoulders and walked off.

"Clarence, tell me what happened tell me everything that you can remember." Clarence closed his eyes and took a long deep breath.

"Ok, here it is." He leaned his head back and then let it back down so that Melinda could see his face.

"I was sitting at the bar, and Jason approached me and asked if we could talk."

While Clarence began to tell his story, he noticed that Melinda had begun scrolling through her phone. It didn't stop him from telling his story, but he made sure he kept his eye on her.

"When he came and asked me that, I told him hell no and I didn't want anything to do with him. He kept trying to talk to me, but I didn't really pay him attention and it began to piss me off."

Melinda's phone began to ring. She answered it and tried to keep her voice as low as possible.

"Yes, we are here." She whispered while staring at Clarence. She then hung up the phone and gave Clarence the ok to continue with his story.

"So, after a while, I saw him walk outside. I followed him out there and we met up face to face in front of his car; words were exchanged and then..."

"Wait a minute, Clarence. I don't mean to cut you off again, but I have to use the restroom."

She jumped up and walked quickly to the ladies room. She stayed in the restroom for quite a while.

"Ok, I'm in the restroom now is the perfect time so just come in and do your job."

She hung up the phone and walked out of the restroom. She made her way back to the table.

"Ok, Clarence, I'm so sorry. Now, continue."

"Yeah, so after a few words were exchanged, I sw."

Two men wearing suits walked into the bar, and Clarence's heart began to pound. They walked up to the bar and spoke with Mr. Rich. Mr. Rich obviously didn't tell them what they wanted to hear, so they turned their attention to the only other people who were inside the bar. One of them stayed and spoke with Mr. Rich, and the other began to walk towards Clarence. As he reached the table, Clarence's heart began to pound even more. The man took off his sunglasses.

"Are you Clarence?" Clarence nodded his head.

"Ok, sir. Well, you're going to have to come downtown, so we can ask you a few questions."

Clarence turned and looked at Melinda. She turned her head because she couldn't stand to look him in the face.

"Melinda, what's going on?" She had no answer for him, and she walked into the back of the bar.

"Come on, sir, we don't have all day."

The two men surrounded Clarence. He didn't expect this to happen to him. With all the other problems he had before Jason's death, this just made his life even worse. The two gentlemen headed for the door, and Clarence followed. They walked to a black car with dark tinted windows. One jumped in the driver's seat, and the other opened the back passenger door for Clarence. Clarence got in the car and dropped his head. The second man closed the door and climbed into the passenger seat, and they drove off. Meanwhile, inside the bar Melinda sat at the table alone. Just shaking her head.

"Melinda."

She heard a man call out her voice. She turned and saw Mr. Rich walking through the front door.

"What's wrong, girl? Why are you sitting there like you just lost your dog or something?" He walked up to the table and sat across from her.

"I just have a few things on my mind, that's all."

"Is there anything you wanna talk about?" She shook her head.

"Well, I'm going to make me drink, do you want one?"

Again, she shook her head. Then, her phone began to vibrate.

She pulled it out and there was a text message that read: "Good job, Melinda. I'll come to see you later on."

She turned the phone over without responding and as soon as she sat the phone down vibrated again.

"He got what he deserved."

The two officers and Clarence arrived at the police station. The driver jumped out stretched and began to walk inside. The officer in the passenger seat got out of the car and opened the door for Clarence. Clarence didn't get out.

"You do know that I'm an officer myself." Clarence glared at the man who opened his door.

"What the hell does that mean to me?"

Clarence then climbed out of the car.

"That means I know how this process works, and I'm not answering any questions without my lawyer."

The officer then closed the car door.

"That's just fine you can sit your ass in here until your lawyer shows up, but just know that we already know what you have done."

He motioned towards the door, and Clarence began to walk in front of him.

"Wait, you don't walk in front of me you walk side by side, sir."

He tried to grab him by the arm, but Clarence snatched his arm away.

"Don't touch me." Clarence snapped at the man.

"Ok, whatever, let's go, son,"

They both walked inside the station. The guy led Clarence to a room with a table and a couple chairs. Clarence walked in and sat down. After about ten minutes of waiting alone the officer who was driving came into the room. He pulled one of the chairs from underneath the table and stared Clarence down before speaking.

"So, Clarence, let's talk." Clarence looked the man in his eyes as he spoke to him.

"About what? I don't even know why I'm here."

"Oh, you don't know, Clarence?" Clarence shook his head.

"Tell me what happened to Jason."

"Jason who?" Clarence responded. Acting as if he had no idea who the officer was talking about.

"Ok, let's start all over, sir."

The officer pulled a box of cigarettes out from his pants pocket. He held the box out to offer Clarence one, but Clarence declined.

"Ok, my name is Detective Adams. I'm not here to do wrong by you, Clarence, but if you work with me, then I'll work with you."

He pulled a lighter out of his shirt pocket and lit his cigarette and puffed a couple times.

"Now, again, let me ask you what happened to Jason." Clarence shrugged his shoulders.

"I don't know who or what you're talking about, sir."

Clarence sarcastically responded. His response angered the officer. He slammed his hand against the table.

"YOU KNOW EXACTLY WHO I'M TALKING ABOUT YOU..." The officer put the cigarette out.

"I'M TALKING ABOUT YOUR BESTFRIEND! I'M TALKING ABOUT YOUR FORMER ROOMMATE! HE'S DEAD, AND I THINK YOU KNOW WHO KILLED HIM!" Clarence shrugged his shoulders again.

"OH, YOU'RE CLUELESS NOW! I'M TALKING ABOUT THE SAME MAN WHO GOT YOUR LITTLE GIRLFRIEND PREGNANT!"

Clarence jumped to his feet and began to rush toward the officer, but his partner who had been watching from the outside hurried into the room to break them up.

"Oh, yeah tough guy, now you know what the hell I'm talking about." The officer had an evil smirk on his face. His partner pushed him out of the door to try and calm him down. Clarence punched the table. He punched it hard, but didn't really feel the pain because of all the adrenaline that was running through his body. He sat down in his chair. As he sat there looking around the room, he began to wonder how the officer knew about Jason and Ashley. He thought the situation between them was all a lie. At least that's what Ashley made him believe. Twenty minutes had went by and, Clarence was still alone in the room. The second officer came into the room.

"So, Clarence, do you need to make a phone call?"

Clarence nodded his head.

"Ok, sir, here's my phone. I'm going to leave you alone while you make that call, but I'll be right back, so you might want to make it quick."

He gave Clarence his cell phone and walked outside of the room. Clarence called Ashley instead of his lawyer.

"Hello" She picked up after the phone rang a couple times.

"Umm, hello, who is this?"

"Ashley, its Clarence."

She jumped to her feet.

"Clarence, where are you? I've been calling your phone."

21

"So, Clarence, you ready to tell us what happened to Jason?" Both of the officers were in the room with Clarence.

"I don't know what you guys are talking about, and I'm not going to answer any questions without my lawyer present."

They both shrugged their shoulders, and one let out a slight chuckle.

"Ok, sir. Well, that's fine we've got all the time in the world."

They both stood up and left the room once again.

Meanwhile, back at Ashley's apartment, she began pacing back and forth in her kitchen. She stopped and stared at the wine bottle sitting on the counter. She really wanted to drink the whole bottle but chose not to because she didn't want to harm the baby. The front door opened, and Brittany walked through.

"Oh my, God, Brittany. I'm glad you're here. I really need to talk to you." Brittany made her way into the kitchen and placed her keys onto the counter.

"What's wrong, Ashley?"

"The police have Clarence downtown for questioning; they think he murdered Jason."

Brittany took a deep breath before she responded. She had to gather her thoughts to make sure she didn't say anything to upset or offend Ashley. It was already hard because Ashley was with child and at the same time the father of her child was being interrogated for the murder of his best friend.

"What would make them think that Clarence had anything to do with it?" She tried her best to sound more concerned than sarcastic.

"I don't know, Brittany, but I hope he knows nothing of it because he needs to be here for his son."

"Oh. My. God. Ashley, you guys are having a boy? I knew it."

She tried to change the subject, but that was impossible for Ashley.

"Have you guys came up with a name?"

"Brittany, I can't even think about that right now. I have to see Clarence. Do you think they're going to keep him down there? I hope he's not afraid. I hope he's warm. I hope they fed him."

Ashley really began to panic as all those thoughts began to run through her mind.

"Ashley, everything will be ok. Maybe they're just trying to scare him, so he'll tell them what they need to know. Clarence is an officer himself; he should know how to handle this situation. I mean, especially if he had nothing to do with it."

That remark caused Ashley to stare her friend up and down.

"And what do you mean by that, Brittany?" Brittany shook her head.

"Are you saying that Clarence had something to do with Jason being killed?"

"I don't know, Ashley, but I mean, let's be realistic. You said it yourself, Clarence had been acting strange."

Brittany walked into the living room. Ashley wasn't too far behind.

"Yeah, he was acting strange, but he would never kill anybody. That's not the Clarence I know."

"I'm not saying he killed him, Ashley, but what if he knows what happened"

Ashley didn't like what she was hearing. She needed her friend to console her. She was expecting her to tell her what she wanted to hear instead of what she needed to hear.

"Please, get out, Brittany."

"What do you mean get out?"

Ashley walked to the front door and opened it.

"I need to be alone."

Brittany walked towards her. She shook her head and left the apartment without saying anything else. Ashley made her way back to the living room and pulled out her cell phone. She scrolled through her contacts and then made a phone call. The phone rang about three times and then a man picked up.

"Hey, Ashley, what's going on/"

"I need to talk to you can you come over"

"Umm, yeah. Sure, just let me finish up a few things here at the house, and I'll be on my way."

"How soon can you get here?"

"Give me about thirty minutes, sweetheart."

"Ok, please hurry."

"Ok, I will but what's wrong, Ash..."

Before he could even finish talking, she hung up the phone. About forty five minutes later, there was a knock on the door. Ashley went to open it. Before she opened the door, she went and put her cell phone on the charger in her room. She then walked back to the door and opened it.

"Took you long enough, I thought maybe you had left or something."

The man standing on the other side of the door was John. Ashley opened the door wide enough for him to walk inside. He began to make his way into the living room. Ashley closed the door and followed behind him.

"So, what's going on, Ashley?" He sat down on the recliner and she sat on the sofa.

"John, I think Clarence is in big trouble." He leaned closer to her.

"Trouble?" He tried his best to sound surprised.

"What kind of trouble, Ashley?"

Tears began to fall from her eyes.

"Well, the police picked him up, and they took him to the station to question him about Jason's death"

"Oh my, God, Ashley. Jason is dead? When did this happen? I mean, how did this happen?"

She was so emotional at the moment she didn't even notice his sarcasm.

"John, I need you to help him, please." John moved from the recliner and sat next to her on the sofa.

"Of course, Ashley, anything you need."

"Well, are you still friends with that good lawyer?" He nodded his head.

"Oh yeah, we're still very close." He wiped the tears as the fell from her eyes. She pulled her head back.

"Ok. Well, can you give him a call and see if he can help?" John pulled out his cell phone.

"I will do that right now." Ashley jumped to her feet. She placed her hand on his shoulder.

"Thank you so much, you're such a great friend." She began to walk to her bedroom.

"I'll be right back, John." she yelled out. John quickly put the phone back into his pocket. Ashley went into the room to see if her phone had any missed calls. While checking her phone she yelled out to John.

"So, did you get in touch with him, John?"

"Uhhh, he didn't answer, but I left him a message. I'm sure he'll call right back; you know how those lawyers can be so busy."

All of a sudden there was a knock at the door.

"John, can you get the door, it's probably Brittany. She must've left her key."

John walked towards the door, and then opened it, and the look on his face would've made you think he saw a ghost.

22

The man on the other side of the door didn't stay to wait for Ashley. He saw who opened the door and took off. John smiled as he saw him walk off.

"John, who is it at the door?" Ashley yelled from the bedroom. John closed the door and headed for her room.

"Oh umm, it was the pizza guy." She looked up from her phone.

"The pizza guy?" She had a puzzled look on her face.

"Yeah, they had the wrong apartment though." John flashed the same grin he had been showing all day.

"I guess."

Ashley responded as she walked out of the room back into the living room. She made sure she brought her phone with her just in case Clarence called for her. John followed behind her and sat back on the sofa.

"So, has your lawyer called you back?" Ashley sat next to him.

"No, not yet, but I'm sure he's just busy right now. Don't worry, Ashley, he's gonna call, and we are gonna get things figured out."

Ashley smiled. She felt relived knowing that John was willing to help her.

"So, John how's your wife and the baby; she's due any day now."

John was caught up staring at Ashley's lips as she talked. He began to day dream.

"JOHN"

Ashley screamed out his name to try and get his attention.

"Huh, oh yeah, yeah. They're great, and yeah uhh any day now."
He tried to regain his focus.

"You alright, John?" John smiled.

"Yeah, of course I'm fine, Ashley."

He moved closer to her and placed his hand on her leg.

"Ashley, there's something that I want to tell you, and I've been wanting to tell you for so long now."

She pulled her leg away from his hand. Ashley didn't know where he was going with what he said, and she began to feel awkward.

"Umm, what do you have to say to me John?" John took a deep breath and then cleared his throat.

"I've missed you so much, Ashley, and to finally see you again after all this time. I realized I made a mistake by letting you get away."

They both stared each other in the eyes as he spoke to her. John stood to his feet and walked into the kitchen.

"John, what are you doing?"

"Do you mind if I make myself something to drink? I'm really thirsty."

"Oh, I guess that's fine."

He went into the fridge and grabbed the bottle of wine that Brittany had opened a couple days before. He then poured himself a glass and drunk it in one gulp. You would've thought it was water the way he took it down so fast. After downing the first glass, he poured himself a second and did the same with that one. John then made his way back into the living room.

"Ok, John, I understand that you may miss me and all, but you're married with a baby on the way and I'm with Clarence. Our time is done."

He sat next to her on the sofa and placed his hand on her leg once again. This time, she didn't move it.

"Ashley, I love my wife don't get me wrong, but I'm still in love with you."

Ashley was shocked. She didn't know how to respond to him. Once again, her hormones began to take over and her emotions were all over the place.

"John, I will always care about you, but like I said, I'm with Clarence and I'm in love with him. I'm sorry."

"It's ok, Ashley. I understand completely. I mean, Clarence is a good guy and all I'm sure you two will be great together, especially when he gets out of jail. How much time do they give you for murder again?"

Ashley's heart dropped. It felt like to her the whole world had stopped after hearing those words come from John's mouth.

"Why would you say something like that, John?" She stood to her feet and walked into the kitchen. He immediately jumped to his feet and followed her. John grabbed her hand and turned her around, so that they were standing face to face. He then grabbed her other hand.

"Ashley, I'm sorry. I wasn't trying to upset you, I promise, but I mean, just what if he did murder Jason? Then what are you gonna do? Are you gonna sit around and let life pass you by waiting for him, or are you going to move on with your life and be happy?"

Ashley had been looking down at the floor as he spoke but after he finished, she picked her head up and looked him in the eyes.

"Be happy, John." He smiled.

"Yes, Ashley, be happy and live life."

"So, I should just be with you and forget all about Clarence; is what you're saying?"

John nodded his head. Ashley smiled at him. John finally felt like he was getting through to her. So, he leaned in for a kiss. Ashley moved her head just in time so John's attempt to kiss her lips was a complete fail

"What's .wrong, Ashley?"

He tried grabbing her hands again. But she pulled away from him.

"John, please get the hell out and don't you ever come back here again. I told you I'm in love with Clarence, and I'm going to stand by his side no matter what. I know that he's innocent."

John shook his head and made his way to the door.

"Don't be too sure about that, sweetheart." He opened the door and walked out and slammed the door behind him.

23

Ashley made her way back into the living room. She heard someone knocking on the door as she began to sit on the sofa.

"JOHN, I ASKED YOU TO LEAVE AND TO NEVER COME BACK! NOW PLEASE LEAVE!"

The knocking continued. She stood up and began to walk to the door.

"JOHN, PLEASE LEAVE BEFORE I HAVE TO CALL THE POLICE!"

She pulled the door open only to see that it wasn't John standing on the other side. The person on the other side of the door happened to be none other than the same woman Ashley saw coming out of Clarence's' apartment. Melinda.

"What are you doing here?" Ashley stared the woman up and down.

"We really need to talk; may I come in?"

"I don't want to talk to you, how did you even know where I lived?"

"Never mind that, Ashley, just let me in. Let's sit down like two adults and talk. I have some things you need to hear."

Again, Ashley hesitated. After looking the woman up and down again, she finally opened the door up and let her in. Melinda walked past her and then turned to face her. Ashley made her way into the living room and then sat on the sofa. Melinda stood still as she watched Ashley get comfortable.

"You're welcome to sit down." Melinda walked over and sat next to Ashley on the sofa.

"Ok, look, we haven't been introduced to each other, and I know you're wondering how I found you, but I'll get into that part later." Ashley stared at Melinda with her arms crossed.

"My name is Melinda, I bartend down at Mr. Rich's bar; that's how I met Clarence." Ashley sat up straight on the sofa and cleared her throat.

"So, were you and Clarence sleeping with each other?" Ashley cut Melinda off before she could finish talking.

"What? What, no, Ashley, never." Ashley didn't believe her. She began to shake her head.

"So, why were you at his apartment the day I first saw you?" Melinda was frustrated with the way Ashley was antagonizing her.

"Look, I came here to try and help you. Just calm down and listen to what I have to say." Ashley nodded her head.

"Me and Clarence never slept together; we aren't and never will be on that level. We developed a friendship. When the two of you were having problems, he would ask for my advice."

Melinda's phone began to ring. She pulled it out of her purse to see who it was and put it back into the purse.

"I told him that he should work things out with you, and he should sit down and talk with you just to have a better understanding on what was really going on."

"You told him that?" Again, Ashley cut Melinda off. This time, she wasn't as aggressive. Melinda nodded her head.

"Clarence really cares about you, and he wants to be with you."

"Ok, so, is this the reason you came over here just to tell me that he cares about me?" Melinda's phone rang once again. This time, when she pulled it out of her purse she answered it.

"Look, I told you I'd call you back when I can. Now, stop calling me." She hung up and tossed her phone back into her purse.

"No, I wanted to talk to you about the whole Jason situation."

Ashley moved closer to Melinda as she spoke. She wanted to let her know that she had her attention. Ashley's phone began to ring. It was from an unknown number, so she didn't answer. Before she could put it down, it rang again. She rejected the call. Hearing what Melinda had to say was more important to her than answering the phone.

"Do you need to take that call?" Melinda asked her as she watched her turn the ringer off on her phone.

"No, I want you to continue."

"Ok, the night Jason was killed, I was at the bar and I saw both him and Clarence talking. Well, it was really more Jason doing all the talking, and Clarence didn't seem too interested in whatever he was trying to say." She coughed and tried clearing her throat.

"Do you mind if I get a glass of water?"

Ashley looked her up and down yet again and then responded, "Yeah, sure, I'll get you some water."

She stood up and walked into the kitchen. While she looked for a cup, Melinda pulled out her cell phone and sent a text message to the person who had been calling her. She hurried and put the phone back into her purse before Ashley made it back to the sofa. Ashley saw her putting the phone back into her purse, but it didn't really bother her. She just wanted Melinda to finish her story. She handed Melinda the glass and sat down on the sofa. Melinda took a sip of the water and cleared her throat.

"After Clarence basically dismissed Jason, I saw Jason walk outside, and then I walked over to Clarence and asked him was everything ok, and I could see in his eyes that he was very angry." She took another sip of the water.

"He then told me that he wanted to kill Jason." Ashley heard those words and just began to shake her head in disbelief.

"Ashley, I tried to calm him down, but it didn't work. He got up from his seat and stormed outside." Ashley's eyes began to water.

"I tried to find Mr. Rich, but he was nowhere in sight, so I ran outside, but it was too late, Clarence had..."

She paused as she heard keys turning in the door. Both she and Ashley's attention turned to the front door. In walked Brittany. Brittany walked into the living room where the two of them were sitting. Before she spoke to Ashley, her and Melinda locked eyes with each other as if they had known each other and had an ongoing beef with each other. Melinda's phone began to ring again. She answered.

"Yes, I know. I'm on the way." she hung up the phone and stood to her feet. She then turned to face Ashley.

"I'm really sorry, Ashley, but I have to run." Ashley climbed to her feet.

"What do you mean you have to run? You haven't finished telling me what happened." Melinda headed for the door very quickly.

"I know. I know, but, umm, my boyfriend has been calling and calling and it's an emergency. I promise, I'll get back with you as soon as possible."

"But you can't..." before Ashley could even finish, Melinda ran out the door and slammed it behind her.

Ashley sat down on the sofa and began to cry. As she was crying, she found herself rubbing her chest again. The pains she had been having had begun to hit her again. All she could do was cry. Brittany walked over and sat next to her. She put her arm around Ashley.

"Ashley, what was she doing here?" Ashley looked up and into Brittany's eyes.

"She came over to give me information on what happened between Clarence and Jason." Her eyes were blood shot and full with tears.

"What do you mean information?" Ashley turned her head from Brittany.

"Ashley, what did she tell you?" Ashley stood up and walked into the kitchen. She grabbed a bottle of wine and filled up a glass. Brittany jumped up and ran into the kitchen.

"Ashley, what are you doing?" Before Ashley took a drink, she looked Brittany into her eyes and just shook her head. She then took down the drink and didn't stop until the glass was empty.

"Ashley, are you crazy? You're pregnant; you shouldn't be drinking."

"It's ok to drink a little wine when you're pregnant, Brittany."

"And who exactly told you that?" Ashley again shook her head and poured herself another glass. Brittany hurried up and snatched the glass from her.

"That's enough, Ashley, what is going on with you?" Ashley tried to grab the glass back from Brittany, but her attempt failed. Brittany ran to the sink and poured out the wine.

"What the hell is wrong with you? That's good wine that you're wasting."

"You don't need to be drinking. Ashley, not right now, you don't." She put the glass into the sink and approached Ashley. Ashley put the bottle down on the kitchen table.

"How could he do this to me, Brittany?"

"Ashley, you have to talk to me, tell me what that bitch told you." Ashley paused.

"Brittany, do you know her?"

"Well, I don't know her exactly, but I think she used to be involved with Jason."

"Wait a minute, what do you mean involved?"

Brittany then walked into the living room. Ashley followed behind her, still rubbing her chest.

"You know what involved means, Ashley, don't act green." They both sat down on the sofa.

"So, she and Jason used to have a relationship is what..."

"They were fuckin, Ashley, screwing, sleeping around."

Ashley's jaw dropped. Definitely wasn't the news she was expecting to hear.

"So, basically you two were sharing Jason." That statement seemed to rub Brittany the wrong way.

"Hell no." She rolled her eyes at Ashley

"I don't share anything. One night, she decided pop up at his house unannounced, and I was the one to answer the door."

"Oh my, God, Brittany. So, what happened when you saw each other?" Brittany pulled out her cell phone checked the time and put it back into her purse.

"Well, just as I opened the door, Jason came out of the bathroom. He tried to downplay things and act like she was just an old friend." Ashley sucked her teeth and shook her head.

"But I knew he was lying because she had an attitude when he introduced her as his old friend."

"Ok, so, what did she even come there for?" Ashley wiped the tears from her eyes as she listened to Brittany tell her story.

"Well, apparently they were more than just friends because after a few minutes, she turned to leave but before she walked out of the door she turned and told Jason that she was pregnant."

Again, that news caused Ashley's mouth to drop. She was at a loss for words.

"Wow, are you serious?" Brittany nodded her head.

"And get this, when she left, I didn't even say a word. He just came out and said he had no idea why she made that statement, and he had never slept with her before."

Brittany's phone began to ring. She picked up the phone and was hesitant to answer at first because she didn't recognize the number. She decided to answer it just before the caller hung up.

"Hello?" No response.

"HELLO!" she yelled but there was still no response. She looked at Ashley, and Ashley did nothing but shrug her shoulders. Brittany could hear someone breathing on the other line, so she waited for them to speak and then they hung up.

"Well, anyways, I guess that's just someone with too much time on their hands." Ashley chuckled. Then, something hit her.

"Wait a minute, Brittany; do you think Melinda had something to do with Jason being killed?"

"You know what, I never even thought about that at first, but maybe so."

"I mean, what if she did it and to clear up her name she set up Clarence."

"Well, tell me what she said when she was here." Ashley paused for a second to try and remember exactly what Melinda said to her.

"All she said was that she saw Jason and Clarence at the bar, and Jason tried to talk to Clarence, but he brushed him off."

Brittany's phone began to ring again. The same number, so she ignored the call.

"She then said Jason left, and she came over to try and talk to Clarence, but he was so angry and said that he wanted to kill Jason."

Brittany's facial expressions quickly changed as she listened to Ashley.

"After she told me that you walked in, and she left."

"This doesn't sound right to me, Ashley. Something just feels weird about that."

Brittany's story about Jason and Melinda made her wonder if Melinda was trying to set Jason up. That's something only Melinda would know. She felt like she had to get to the bottom of it. As she sat there next to Brittany, she kept feeling the pains in her chest.

"What's going on with your chest, Ashley, you keep rubbing it."

"Just a little heartburn, nothing major." Brittany's face was full of concern.

"Uh huh, well..." Ashley's phone began to ring. It just so happened to be the same Number that had called Brittany's phone.

"Hello?" Ashley said as soon as she answered the call. "All you had to do was keep your mouth shut."

24

Ashley stared at her phone for a few seconds. She sat and tried to figure out who it was on the phone.

"Umm, Ashley, who was that on the phone?" Brittany asked.

"I don't know, Brittany."

"Well, damn, what did they say? You're sitting there looking like they told you your best friend died, and seeing that I'm sitting right here, that can't be the case."

Brittany tried to make light of the situation to try and get her friend to laugh, but it didn't work.

"All they said was you should've kept your mouth shut." Brittany's facial expression changed as soon as she heard those words.

"Really, and you don't know who it was?" Ashley shook her head.

"Well, call the number back duh, Ashley." Ashley called the number back, and it rang a few times, but no one answered. She called twice more. Same result.

"Let me see the phone, Ashley. I'll call them from mine."

Ashley handed her the phone, and Brittany began to enter the number into her phone. She paused before she called the number.

"Wait a minute, Ashley; this is the same number that called me earlier." They looked at each other.

"Well, who do you think it is, Brittany?" Brittany shrugged her shoulders.

"I have no idea, but we're going to find out."

She then called the number. Again there was no response.

"Obviously, it's somebody who knows both of us, and now they're not gonna answer because they know we're together."

Brittany was determined to find out who it was calling both her and Ashley. She kept calling and calling. Maybe about five or six times, and there was still no answer.

"Well, damn, Brittany, how many times do you plan on calling?"

She picked her phone up from the coffee table. Ashley was still rubbing her chest. She then felt movements in her stomach.

"Oh my, God, Brittany."

Brittany didn't turn all of her attention to Ashley. As she was still trying to call the number. She gave Ashley the side eye.

"What, Ashley, I'm gonna keep calling until whomever it..."

"No, I'm not talking about that. I just felt the baby kick."

Brittany then turned to face Ashley. She was excited, so she moved closer to Brittany and placed her hand on her stomach.

"Oh my, God. Ashley where is he? I want to feel him."

Ashley grabbed Brittany's hand and placed it where she felt the kicks. She held her hand there for a minute or two.

"I don't feel anything."

"Just wait, I think he's gonna move again."

After another minute, the baby kicked again.

"Aww, Ashley. I felt him kick, it feels so weird."

They both laughed. Ashley's phone began to ring. This time it was from a different number. She looked at Brittany and Brittany gave her a look to let her know she should answer it. And so she did.

"Hello who is this?" At first there was no response.

"Hello Ashley can you hear me?" She pulled the phone away to take another look at the number to see if she could recognize it.

"Yes I can hear you but who is this"

"Ashley it's me Clarence" She gasped. Brittany stared at her as she talked on the phone.

"Oh my God Clarence where are you?"

"I'm on my way home Ashley I had to get me a new phone where are you baby?" Ashley's heart dropped.

"Clarence I'm at home come over here I really need to see you" Clarence paused before he responded.

"Umm ok baby I have some business to take care of first and then as soon as I'm done I'll come straight to you" Ashley sucked her teeth and then let out a heavy sigh.

"Really Clarence I've been losing my mind wondering what's going on with you and you won't come over to see me"

Clarence noticed the frustration in her voice.

"Ashley calm down it won't even take long I just have to get things situated baby I promise I'll be there as soon as I'm finished"

Ashley was upset but she was relieved to finally hear from him.

"Ok Clarence just hurry up"

"Ok baby I'm coming" That put a smile on her face.

"Oh Clarence guess what?"

"What's up Ashley?" Before she responded she began to rub her chest again.

"The baby started kicking today" Clarence's face lit up.

"Aww man I hate I missed his first kick"

"I know Clarence me too but just make sure you don't miss anything else please"

Clarence was unsure how to respond to her. Luckily they were on the phone so she couldn't see it on his face.

"I promise baby I won't miss anything else everything is going to be ok"

He tried his best to sound positive and give her some hope.

"I'll call you when I'm on my way Ashley I love you"

"I love you too Clarence"

They both hung up the phone. Ashley had a smile on her face and Clarence's face showed he was more worried than happy. He then made another phone call. As soon as the person on the other line picked up Clarence didn't waste any time.

"Hey I'm on the way I'll be there in ten minutes"

He didn't give the person a chance to respond. Ashley kept feeling the pains in her chest so she had Brittany drive her to the emergency room. She sat in the room waiting for a doctor to come and check on her. Brittany had to wait for her in the waiting room. The doctor then walked into the room.

"Hello ma'am how are you doing today"

Ashley looked at the doctor and tried to smile. She barely could grin the pain had worsened.

"Well I'm actually in a lot of pain it's all in my chest" The doctor watched her as she moved her hands in a circular motion across her chest.

"Uh huh I see and how far along are you with your pregnancy ma'am"

"I just made 19 weeks sir" He pulled out his clipboard and jotted down a few notes.

"Ok and is this your first pregnancy"

"Yes sir it is" Again he wrote down a few words.

"At first I thought it was just gas or maybe heartburn but it keeps getting worse"

"And about how long have you been experiencing these pains" She moved her hand from her chest and put it on her knee.

"Well it's been going on for maybe a week or two now it started out real mild but like I said the pain has been getting worse and worse"

The doctor continued to write down notes and nod his head as she spoke. He then pulled out his stethoscope. He placed it on to her chest and listened for a couple of seconds. After that he asked her to stand and he stood in front of her.

"Please hold your arms out for me."

She held her arms out and he began to touch the top of her chest. She grimaced as he went over the spots that had been giving her trouble. He then moved his hands down and began to press against her breasts. Again she tried to hold back but the pains were really getting to her.

"Ouch"

"Oh I'm sorry ma'am didn't mean to press down that hard" She shook her head.

"Oh no it wasn't you doctor it's just those same old pains"

"Ok well we're going to run some x-rays and a few other tests so we can see exactly what it is you're welcome to lay on the bed and I'll be right back"

The doctor left and was gone for a while. Ashley had begun to doze off while waiting and then she heard him walk back into the room. He then asked her to get up from the bed and follow him into another room so they could run more tests. After doing the x-ray he took her back into the room where he had her wait yet again. After an hour the doctor came back into the room. He had a concerned look on his face.

"Now don't be alarmed but after running the tests and taking a look at your x-ray results…."

Ashley left the room and met up with Brittany in the waiting room after hearing the devastating news.

"So what did he say Ashley?"

Brittany jumped out of her seat and walked towards Ashley. She put her arm around her to try and comfort her.

"Oh he just said that I need to stop eating greasy food because it's causing me to have frequent heartburn"

Brittany couldn't tell if she was lying because she had a grin on her face. Ashley didn't want her friend to know how serious her situation was so she downplayed it and told her that the doctor said it was only heartburn.

"Ok Ashley well I'll make sure that you eat nothing but salads"

She laughed while Ashley looked the other way to try and hide her frustration. There were a million thoughts running through her mind all at once.

"So how's my God son doing in there is he ok"

"Yes he's fine Brittany can we just go home I'm tired and I wanna lay down"

Brittany nodded her head and they both walked out of the hospital into the parking lot. Meanwhile Clarence made his way to Mr. Rich's bar to try and figure out what was going on. As soon as he walked inside he saw Mr. Rich sitting down at a table by himself. He had his back towards the door so he didn't see Clarence walk in. He walked in front of Mr. Rich and pulled out a chair from under the table and sat down. They both stared each other down before either one of them said anything.

"How are you doing son?"

Mr. Rich reached into his shirt pocket and pulled out a box of cigarettes. He pulled out a cigarette and then held the box in front of Clarence. He wasn't the type to smoke cigarettes but he had so much on his mind he felt that would help calm his nerves. First he hesitated but then he reached inside the box and pulled out a cigarette. Mr. Rich had been smoking for almost half of his life. It was a mystery how he never developed any kind of cancer the way he just ran through two or three boxes per day. Mr. Rich reached into his pants pocket and pulled out a lighter and handed it to Clarence. Clarence struggled with trying to light his cigarette so Mr. Rich reached in and grabbed the lighter back from him and lit his cigarette then he lit Clarence's'.

"So like I asked kid how are you holding up?"

Clarence took a few puffs from his cigarette and then began to choke after the smoke had built up in his throat.

"It's not like you're smoking them damn plants you young folks like to smoke nowadays boy take your time"

He leaned back in his chair and laughed as Clarence struggled with his cigarette. It wasn't doing much for Clarence so he took the cigarette and put it down on the ashtray that was sitting right in front of Mr. Rich.

"I'm not doing too well Mr. Rich it feels like there's so much going on that I don't know about and it's making me lose my mind"

"Son you know things aren't looking too good for you"

He then put his cigarette down and reached for a glass that was halfway empty sitting on the table. He drank the rest and then sat it back down and reached on the ground for a bottle that was sitting next to his chair.

"Whiskey ain't never did me nothing wrong"

Mr. Rich yelled out as he poured another glass.

"You want a taste of this here boy it'll put some hair on that bird chest you got underneath all them shirts you're wearing"

Clarence tried to laugh but everything that was on his mind wouldn't allow him to even crack a smile.

"Sure thing" He replied.

Mr. Rich then whistled and about a minute later a young woman walked out from the back. She was wearing a red blouse that just so happened to be missing a few buttons around her cleavage area.

"Hey Clarence I want you to meet my new bartender her name is Karen"

Clarence smiled and waved at the woman.

"Karen this here's Clarence I been knowing him since he was a little snot nose"

He laughed and so did the woman. She was much more attractive than Melinda. Maybe the reason Mr. Rich hired her.

"So Mr. Rich what happened to?"

Clarence stopped as he realized Mr. Rich was giving him a look to keep his mouth shut.

"Umm Karen honey get Clarence here a glass of milk since he's so much of a pussy cat"

Again he let out a loud chuckle. He then began to cough.

"Only jokes baby girl bring the man whatever he wants"

"And what would you like Clarence?" She flashed her big beautiful smile at Clarence. He caught himself staring at the woman as she waited for his request. He felt Mr. Rich kick his leg underneath the table.

"Oh umm yeah let me get a Jack Daniels"

The woman smiled and nodded her head. Before she turned to walk off Clarence yelled out

"Oh and no ice please!" She then turned and walked to the bar.

"Mr. Rich what happened to Melinda?" Mr. Rich took a drink from his glass and then sat it back on the table.

"She just went crazy man" Clarence's face was full of confusion.

"After that shit happened with Jason she came in here and just lost it I mean really lost it she was drinking on the job, messing up peoples drinks, and one night just started screaming out a bunch of crazy shit"

185

"Crazy shit like what"

They both got quiet as Karen came back to the table with Clarence's drink.

"Do you need anything else Clarence?" Again she smiled at him and again Clarence caught himself staring at her.

"No sweetheart we should be good for now just bring him the bottle just in case he needs another drink"

Karen was younger than Melinda and had a bit more sex appeal. She had long dark hair that came a little past her shoulders. Her body was definitely an eye opener. Clarence's mouth was wide open has he watched her walk back to the bar.

"Look son I know she's a looker but you have way more important things to worry about you have to get your name cleared because this shit isn't just gonna go away this is something serious son and I don't know how you're gonna do it but you need to now I know you had nothing to do with it but those people don't know you like I do"

Clarence sighed and took another drink.

"I don't know what to do Mr. Rich I mean those police seemed to know so much about me and I have no idea how" Mr. Rich shook his head.

"You need to find that bitch Melinda she knows what the hell is going on and I think she's been working with that uptight son of a bitch John but don't quote me because I only know what my eyes tell me"

Clarence finished off his drink and then watched as Mr. Rich stood to his feet.

"Now I need to go and call my wife damn lady been complaining bout back pains I don't know what she expects me to do she thinks I'm some kind of misogynist"

"Umm Mr. Rich don't you mean?"

Mr. Rich stared Clarence down "Never mind"

"Don't go trying to correct me boy I know what the hell I meant"

He obviously had too many drinks because his words began to slur and he basically wasn't making any sense. Clarence sat there and watched Mr. Rich walk into the back. Karen made her way back to the table with the bottle Mr. Rich asked her to bring back.

"Here you go sir" She sat the bottle on the table and began to walk off but before she could Clarence grabbed her by the arm.

"Why don't you have a seat and keep me company for a little while?" She smiled and then turned and took a seat.

Before Clarence began to speak his phone vibrated. It was a text message from Ashley.

"Clarence where are you? There's something I really need to talk to you about"

He read the message but didn't respond. He then turned off his phone and put it into his pocket. Clarence sat with Karen and the two of them flirted with each other for about an hour.

"Well Clarence I'll be getting off soon but I really enjoyed talking to you maybe I'll see you around" Clarence smiled.

"Yeah that would be nice"

She got up and walked to the back to grab her purse and to say goodbye to Mr. Rich. As she walked back out she waved goodbye to

Clarence and made her way to the parking lot. Clarence jumped up and chased after her.

"HEY KAREN!" he yelled out before she got into her car. He ran to her car.

"I was thinking maybe we could hang out for a little while" She smiled.

"I'd really like that umm I wasn't going to do anything tonight just pop some popcorn and watch a few movies"

"That sounds fun I'd love to join you" They both smiled at each other.

"Ok Clarence well I guess just follow me" She got into her car and he ran and jumped into his and then followed her out of the parking lot.

25

Clarence and Karen both made it to her apartment. Clarence still hadn't turned on his cell phone. He was a little buzzed from the drinks he had at the bar but he was still able to function. Karen parked her car and Clarence parked about two spots down from hers. He sat in the car and looked around the parking lot. Her apartment was actually about five minutes away from Ashley's. Clarence was stuck day dreaming while sitting in his car until he heard her tap on the window. It caught him by surprise so when he heard it he jumped. She stood on the outside of the car with her hands in the air smiling.

"Are you getting out or not?" She yelled through the window. Clarence then opened up his door and then got out of the car.

"I'm sorry I was waiting for you"

"Oh ok well come on let's go"

He looked around the apartments and then followed behind her. They made their way to the second floor where her apartment was. She unlocked the door and Clarence walked in behind her.

"Sorry there isn't much in here I just moved in and I'm waiting to get the rest of my furniture out of storage"

There was a sofa sitting against the wall and a big screen TV in front of it mounted on the wall.

"Looks like you have all the things you need to me" Clarence said jokingly.

"Just like a man" She walked into the kitchen area.

"I have some wine Clarence would you like some"

"Uhh yeah sure"

She reached into the refrigerator and pulled out a bottle that had yet to be open. She found a corkscrew and tried to open it but she didn't have much luck. Clarence noticed that she was having a hard time so he jumped up from the sofa and walked into the kitchen.

"Maybe you should let me help you out there" She handed him the bottle and within a few seconds he popped the cork. He looked at Karen and smiled.

"Sometimes it just takes a man's touch" She smiled back at him.

"Oh whatever Clarence" she took the bottle from him and reached into her cabinet and pulled out two wine glasses and filled them both up. Clarence made his way back to the sofa and sat down. She followed him the the two glasses in hand. She sat next to him on the sofa. She handed him his glass and then held hers out.

"Cheers to new friends" They both smiled. Clarence repeated.

"Cheers to new friends" They made a toast and began to drink the wine.

"So Clarence what type of movies do you like?"

"I really like suspense and action movies" She turned on the TV

"Ok well let me see if I can find something for us to watch"

While she flipped through the channels Clarence pulled out his phone and turned it on. As soon as it came on there were back to back messages from Ashley.

"Clarence please just call me I'm really not feeling good and I need you here with me" The second message read.

"Clarence I went to the doctor today I need to tell you about that"

He looked at the phone and thought about texting her back but he didn't. He put the phone back into his pocket. Karen finished off her wine and got up to fix her another glass. She looked at Clarence and noticed he hadn't finished his.

"What's wrong Clarence? You don't want the wine?" He looked down at his glass and then finished it off.

"I'm sorry I forgot all about it"

"Would you like another glass?"

He held out his glass. Instead of having to walk back and forth she brought the whole bottle into the living room. She poured him another glass and the sat it next to her on the sofa. Eventually she found a movie that both of them agreed on. Ashley and Brittany were just sitting around at Ashley's apartment.

"Ashley has he called you back or even responded to any of your messages" She just shook her head.

"I just hope he hasn't gotten into any more trouble Brittany I really need him here with me" She began to cry again.

"I just hate the way all of this has played out Brittany I mean having a baby is supposed to be a blessing so why do I feel like everything has gone wrong since I found out I was pregnant"

Brittany put her arm around Ashley and wiped the tears from her face.

"Brittany sometimes I feel like I've made a big mistake I mean it's like he doesn't love me like he doesn't want anything to do with me"

Brittany was at a loss for words. She just continued to hold her.

"Ashley don't worry he's going to come around Clarence loves you"

Back at Karen's apartment the mood was the exact opposite. Karen just so happened to finish the bottle of wine off herself. She began to fill he buzz come along. She turned to face Clarence who was so focused on the movie. She then leaned in and began to rub his ear. First he pulled back.

"What's wrong Clarence are you shy" He shook his head.

"Don't worry Clarence I don't bite"

She continued to rub on his ear. This time he didn't move. She leaned in and began to kiss him on his neck. She got up from the sofa and stood in front of Clarence. He looked her up and down. She then sat on his lap and they began to kiss. Clarence's phone began to ring and the vibration caused Karen to jump. He reached into his pocket and pulled out his phone. It was Ashley calling him again.

"Do you need to answer that?"

He tossed the phone to the other side of the sofa and pulled her back down and began to kiss her again. Karen pulled off her top and walked into the bedroom. Clarence was a footstep behind her.

26

Ashley had grown tired of trying to reach Clarence. She went into her room to lay down. It wasn't easy for her to fall asleep so she just laid in the bed and stared at the ceiling. Brittany sat in the living playing with her phone. Ashley's phone began to ring. She jumped up to grab it because she expected it to be Clarence but it wasn't. It was the same number that had called her and Brittany.

"WHO THE HELL IS THIS?"

She said as soon as she answered the phone. She heard the person breathing on the other end of the phone.

"Hel..."

"It's John Ashley before you hang up just give me five minutes of your time"

Ashley almost hung up but she decided to give him a chance to say what he had to say.

"Hello" He was trying to make sure that she didn't hang up.

"John I'm waiting for you to say what you have to say" He took a deep breath.

"Ok Ashley I know things look bad and I know things ended on a bad note the last time I was there I just wanted to apologize for coming on to you I just couldn't help myself"

Ashley pulled the phone from the side of her face to see how much time had passed. They had been on the phone for about three minutes.

"You have two minutes John"

"Ok Ashley I just needed to get that off my chest I hope that you aren't upset and able to forgive me because I really want to..."

She cut him off before he could finish.

"Ok John it's been five minutes I'd appreciate it if you didn't contact me or my friend ever again"

Before she hung up she heard him yell out.

"Wait Ashley please don't hang up yet"

"John I have nothing else to say to you first you come over here and try to come on to me knowing I'm with Clarence and then you send me a message saying I should have just kept my mouth shut whatever the hell that means I don't know but I don't want to see you or hear from you ever again now goodbye"

"Wait Ashley Melinda set Clarence up"

Just before she hit the end button her heart dropped as she heard his confession.

"What the hell do you mean she set him up?"

John seemed desperate so he had to do whatever it took to keep her from hanging up.

"Hello John don't get quiet now tell me what the hell you mean"

She pulled the phone away from her face to make sure he didn't hang up.

"Ok Ashley look I don't know who killed Jason but I know that she called the police and told them that it was Clarence and she tried to make me go along with the accusation for some odd reason she had some kind of issue with Jason and she knew that him and Clarence weren't on good terms, so that's why she told the police that it was Clarence to try and cover herself."

Ashley couldn't believe what she was hearing. She really didn't know if she could believe if it were true, but it did make sense. Brittany did tell her that Melinda and Jason had a bad fall out, so maybe that was her just trying to get her revenge. But could she really trust John's word?

"How do I know that you're telling the truth, John?"

"Ashley, I wouldn't dare lie to you; she told me that if I didn't work with her then she'd have the same thing done to me. I mean, how could I say no? I have a wife and a baby on the way."

Ashley sat on the phone shaking her head and rubbing her chest.

"John, I have to call you back."

She didn't give him a chance to respond. She hung up the phone and called Clarence again. Still she couldn't get a hold of him. Instead of giving up, she called back to back.

"Come on, Clarence, please pick up the phone."

She stood up and looked into the living room to see Brittany sleeping on the sofa. She sent Clarence a text message after not being able to reach him via phone call.

"Clarence, I hope that you didn't go and do anything stupid but, baby, I love you and there are some things that I need to talk to you about, so please, just call me back. Please, just let me know that you're ok."

Meanwhile, Clarence and Karen, who had both been drinking throughout the night, were feeling the effects of the wine. Clarence picked her up and gently laid her on her bed. They were so into it. There was a lot of heavy breathing and moaning coming from the bedroom.

"Clarence, I love the way your lips feel."

Clarence smiled at her. They continued to kiss. Karen was beyond turned on by the way he kissed and touched her. She began to take his shirt off. Clarence didn't stop her either. He reached down and began to take her underwear off.

"Wait, Clarence, do you have protection?"

He stopped before he got her panties past her knees.

"Of course I do."

He then reached into his pants pockets. There was nothing. So, then he pulled out his wallet to see if there was one inside, and again there was nothing. So, he looked at her and frowned.

"No, Clarence. I want to feel you inside of me."

He dropped down on the bed and laid next to her. She sighed and then climbed on top of him.

"I guess it wasn't meant to be."

Clarence said jokingly. But Karen was so turned on, she couldn't resist. She began to kiss him again. She went from his lips to his neck. She reached down into his pants and began to stroke him slowly. She took her panties off and then pulled down his pants. Just as she began to insert his penis inside of her he screamed out.

"ASHLEY, WAIT!" She stopped and climbed off him.

"Who the hell is Ashley?"

Clarence sat on the edge of the bed and stared at the floor. He knew that he had really messed up. He couldn't believe that he put himself in a position to do something that he would regret for such a long time.

"Clarence, who is Ashley?"

He took a while to respond. He continued to sit on the edge of the bed twitching his fingers. She stood up and walked to the end of the bed and sat next to him. She then placed her hand on his leg.

"I'm sorry, Karen. I should've never come here, it's not right."

"What do you mean, Clarence, what's wrong?" Clarence shook his head.

"I have a girlfriend Karen"

Karen laughed at his confession. He turned and looked at her to see what she thought was funny.

"Why are you laughing?" She looked at Clarence and continued to smile.

"Clarence, I know you have a girlfriend." Her response caught Clarence off guard.

"How did you know that? I mean, we just met." He sat and wondered how she could've known about him having a girlfriend.

"I know Mr..."

"No, Clarence Mr. Rich didn't tell me anything" Clarence stood to his feet.

"Well how did you know?"

"Clarence some guy came into the bar a few times talking about you" He turned and faced her.

"Wait a minute what's this guy's name?" She shrugged her shoulders.

"Clarence, I don't know his name. I never even asked; all he said was that he was looking for you, and that he knew your girlfriend very well."

By now, Clarence was beyond confused.

"I don't understand this at all, Karen, what else did he say to you?"

"Well, not much besides that."

Clarence stared her up and down. He felt like there was more to it and he needed answers.

"Every time he came in the bar, he would act so strange."

"What do you mean strange?"

Karen stood up and walked into her restroom which was connected to the bedroom. She came back into the bedroom wearing a long black robe.

"It's like he didn't want anyone to see him, and whenever Mr. Rich would come around, he'd duck off and leave the bar."

Who could it have been? Clarence didn't know what to think. He pulled up his pants and began to put his shirt back on.

"Are you leaving, Clarence?" He looked her in the face and nodded his head.

"Karen, there is so much going on right now. I have to go."

He walked out of the bedroom and headed towards the door.

"Clarence, are you sure you want to leave upset like this? I mean, you've been drinking and it's three in the morning."

Just as he reached the door, he turned and asked her.

"This guy, is there anything else he said to you about me?"

She shook her head. Clarence turned and began to open the door. Before he walked out, he turned and gave her a kiss. She couldn't help but smile. The kiss felt so good. Clarence wrapped his arms around her waist and pulled her closer to him. They kissed for about five minutes. Clarence then pulled back.

"I'm so sorry, Karen, I have to go. I'll talk to you later."

He then walked out of the apartment and ran down the steps. Karen walked back into her apartment with a grin on her face. Clarence ran to his car and started the engine. Before he drove off, he pulled out his cell phone and called Ashley. She didn't pick up the first time, so he called again. Still, there was no answer. He threw the phone into the passenger seat and pulled out of the parking lot then headed for her apartment. It wasn't a long drive because Ashley was almost within walking distance of where Karen lived. As soon as he made it to her apartment, he found a parking spot and jumped out of the car.

Before he walked away from his car, he realized that he left his phone inside. He opened the door and grabbed it and called Ashley's phone again. She didn't answer. He chose to go to her apartment anyway. As he made it to her door, he stood and tried to think of an excuse for why he ignored all of her phone calls and messages. He then began to knock on the door. After a few knocks, there was still no answer. He stood and waited to see if Ashley would come, but she didn't. So, he began to head towards the steps until he heard someone open the door. Only it wasn't Ashley, it was Brittany who answered the door. She yawned as she stood in the door way.

"Clarence, you really have some nerve."

He walked up to the door and tried to walk in, but she stood in his way.

"Brittany, what are you doing? Let me in."

"Why should I let you in?" Clarence sucked his teeth and shook his head.

"I need to talk to Ashley, now please"

"Brittany who is that at the door?"

Ashley woke up as she heard the two of them going back and forth.

"Well, she doesn't want to talk to you."

She closed the door in his face just as Ashley made her way out of her room.

"Oh, Ashley, those were just the neighbors asking to use a flashlight. I told them you didn't have one."

Clarence began to knock on the door again.

"Brittany why would you tell them that? Of course I have a flashlight they can use."

She walked past Brittany and opened the door. Only to see Clarence standing on the other side. They both stared at each other. Brittany was expecting Ashley to yell at Clarence, but she witnessed the exact opposite.

"Clarence, where have you been? I've been worried sick, baby." She said in a very gentle and calm manner.

"Ashley, we have to talk."

She let him inside of the apartment. They both began to walk inside of her bedroom.

"Wait a minute, where are you guys going?"

Brittany yelled out. She seemed concerned, but she really wanted to be nosey. Ashley wasn't falling for it though.

"Brittany, goodnight, we're going to sleep."

She closed her bedroom door, and Brittany dropped down onto the sofa. Clarence sat on the side of the bed and Ashley sat next to him.

"Ashley, I'm sorry. I left my phone at my apartment, and I went to talk to Mr. Rich."

Ashley was just so happy that nothing had happened to him. She began to rub his head.

"It wasn't until after about an hour or so that I realized I left my phone at home. Well, actually, I thought I lost it at the bar."

"Clarence, it's ok. I'm just glad you're here and in one piece."

There was no way that he could tell her the truth. So, he chose to tell half of the story instead of the whole story. Which most women would refer to as a lie.

"Ashley, I saw your message saying that you really needed to talk to me; what's wrong?"

Ashley was so nervous to tell him the news that the doctor had given her.

"Well...." she stared into his eyes, and the words just wouldn't come out. She was more afraid to tell him than she was to hear the news herself.

"Remember when I told you that I wanted to be married with a child?" Clarence nodded his head.

"Well, I've just been thinking about that a lot lately, Clarence."

He was at a loss for words. Clarence could still smell the perfume of another woman on the top of his lip as he sat there and had to discuss marriage with the woman who was carrying his unborn child. Again both of them sat in each other's face and held in important information. Both of them stared into each other's eyes knowing they had secrets that would just kill one another inside.

27

"Marriage?" Clarence repeated the word as he began to scratch his head.

"Yes, Clarence. I mean, I don't want to be just another statistic."

She moved closer to him and placed her head on his shoulder. Clarence stared at the wall trying to figure out the right words to say. He really loved Ashley and was excited about the two of them having a child together, but he wasn't too sure about marriage. Although he wanted to do whatever it took to keep Ashley happy, there many issues he had to face. As he sat there wondering how he could explain to her where he had been all night. The woman he spent his night with had information that he felt Ashley should know, but how he'd explain to her how he found out was the dilemma.

"Clarence."

He shook his head as his mind raced, and he stared at the wall day dreaming.

"Yes, baby?"

"So, what do you think about it?" She pulled her head away from his shoulder and looked him in his eyes awaiting his response.

"Think about what?"

He tried to pretend as if he didn't hear her, which struck a nerve with her.

"REALLY, CLARENCE?"

She stood up and tried to storm out of the room, but he grabbed a hold of her arm before she reached the door.

"What's wrong, Ashley? I'm so sorry; my mind is all over the place." She turned to face him and folded her arms across her chest

"Well, right now, Clarence, I need your mind here with me." He pulled her back to the bed, and she sat next to him.

"I was asking you about marriage, Clarence; don't you think we should be discussing that?"

"Umm..." Ashley gave him a side eye.

"Yeah, I guess. I mean, that's something we should take a look at."

His responses seemed so dry to her.

"Clarence, what exactly is going on? You seem like something is bothering you. I mean, do you not love me like you used to? It's like lately you've been acting so strange."

By this time, Clarence was annoyed by what he felt was her nagging him.

"What the hell do you mean strange, Ashley?" He jumped up from the bed.

"My friend was killed and I happen to be a suspect and you're sitting her talking about me acting strange are you kidding me?" His frustration had begun to show as he paced back and forth.

"Clarence, I wasn't trying to..." He cut her off before she could finish.

"And then here you are on my back, talking about marriage. How can I sit here and think about that when I'm facing the shit I'm facing? It's like all you think about is yourself."

Ashely sat and listened to Clarence go on his rant. She felt something vibrating next to her. When Clarence jumped up from the bed, his phone fell out of his pocket. He stopped pacing and looked at Ashley as she began to cry.

"I'm sorry, Ashley. I didn't mean to yell at you, I'm just so frustrated right now."

"And you don't think I am, Clarence? I mean, what the hell is going on? Tell me the truth, did you kill Jason?" Clarence was surprised that she could even ask him such a thing.

"What, how could you even ask me that?" His phone began to vibrate. He had no idea that his phone wasn't in his pocket.

"Look, I need to use the bathroom."

He walked into the bathroom and closed the door. Ashley picked up his phone, and there were text messages from a number that hadn't been saved. She debated for a quick second whether she should read them or not but chose to do so because she needed answers. She wanted to know what Clarence really had going on.

The first message read: "Clarence, even though the night didn't end the way I would have liked it to, I really did enjoy your company."

Reading that first message caused Ashley's heart to drop to her stomach. She covered her mouth with her hand as she read the second message.

"And I just love the way your lips feel I guess I'll just have to..." Ashley dropped the phone as she heard Clarence opening the bathroom door.

"Ashley, listen. I'm really sorry for the way I just talked to you, baby, you know I didn't mean any harm, it's just..." He stopped as he saw her crying and shaking her head.

"Get out, Clarence." Clarence had no idea that she had gone through his phone and read his messages.

"Why, Ashley?" She stood up and grabbed his phone.

"Maybe you need to call whoever this person is texting your phone and ask them why." Clarence knew he messed up.

"Ashley, look you have the wrong idea. Now, I don't know what you saw or what you think you saw, but whatever it is, you have to understand I haven't done anything wrong."

She threw the phone, and it hit Clarence in his chest.

"Please, just get out of here; you're such a liar. Everything you've ever told me has been a lie. You don't love me; you've been lying to me this whole time."

He picked up his phone and walked towards her. She pushed him away.

"How could you sit here and lie to my face like that, Clarence? I trusted you and all this time. I've been afraid that I'd lose you because of the whole Jason situation, and you're out with another woman."

"Wait a minute, Ashley, it's not like that. I promise." She walked towards the door.

"Who is she, Clarence?" Clarence didn't even look at his phone to see who had sent the messages.

"Is it Melinda?" He shook his head as he approached her.

"Ashley, no. I promise you, whatever you read, it's just a misunderstanding. Hell, whoever it is probably had the wrong number."

"CALL HER!"

His mouth dropped. He had no idea what to do or say.

"Don't just stand there, Clarence, let's just find out if she had the wrong number." She said sarcastically.

"I want you to call her and put her on speaker phone." Clarence didn't budge.

"Well since you can't do it get the hell out and don't ever come back. I don't need you."

"Ok, Ashley. I'll call her."

He hesitated for about a minute before he called. His hands were sweaty and shaking as he called the number. He held it up to his face.

"I said put it on speaker."

Clarence almost dropped the phone he was so nervous. The phone continued to ring as he put it on speaker. After about a few rings it stopped. Clarence thought it was going to voicemail because there was a short silence. He had no idea that Karen had answered the phone.

"Hey, baby, did you have a change of heart? If so, I'm still in the same position you left me in."

Clarence didn't even respond. He just hung up the phone.

"The wrong number, huh?"

Ashley was so disgusted with him. Clarence was stuck. He didn't know what to say, but he knew he had to do something. He felt the need to plead his case.

"Ashley, I promise you it's not what you think."

She turned her back to him. He walked up to her and placed his hand on the back of her shoulder. She pulled away from him.

"Don't touch me."

"Ashley, I promise you, I didn't do anything with her. I only went over there because she told me she had some information on what happened to Jason. I had to go because I felt I needed to at least hear her out." Ashley began to cry even harder.

"Ashley, she's a new bartender down at Mr. Rich's bar, and she means not..." Ashley turned to him and punched him in his eye before he could finish. Clarence put a hand over his eye.

"Ok, Ashley. I know you're mad, but just listen to me. I love you, and I want to be with you."

"Clarence, get out now. Please, just leave."

To avoid being hit again, Clarence walked out of the room. He stopped before walking out the apartment. Ashley came out of the room behind him. They stared each other down for a few minutes without saying a word. Brittany was still sleep on the sofa. Neither one of them wanted to wake her, so Clarence opened the door and walked out. Ashley went back into the bed room and cried herself to sleep. The next morning, Brittany came into Ashley's room to check on her. She walked in to see Ashley sitting on the floor next to her bed still crying. She sat next to her on the floor.

"What's wrong, Ashley?"

"I had a feeling that something was going on, Brittany. I just knew it, but my heart didn't want me to believe that he would ever hurt me."

Brittany shook her head.

"That's how it always is, Ashley, all these men are the same; they start off sweeping us off our feet, and then after they get what they really want, they use the dust pan to put us into the trash can."

She laughed a little. Ashley wasn't too fond of her strange theory.

"But he just seemed like the perfect man, and now it really makes me question whether he's ever told me the truth."

"Ashley, what happened exactly?"

She stood up and sat on the bed. Ashley remained on the floor. Being pregnant and all, she figured it would take her a little longer to get up, so she chose to stay put.

"The whole night he was with another woman, Brittany; he lied to me and told me that he was at the bar all night, but he was really with some woman."

"And how do you know that, Ashley?"

Ashley had enough of sitting on the floor. Her back was beginning to hurt. She reached back to try and pull herself up on the bed, but it was a struggle, so Brittany had to give her a hand. By the time she was able to get back on the bed she was out of breath.

"I read a text message she sent and then I had him call her and she answered saying I'm still in the position you left me in"

Brittany's jaw dropped.

"WOW! Are you serious" Ashley nodded her head.

"And what did he say?"

"What the hell could he say? Brittany, he was caught in his lie. I mean, he tried to say something about her having information about Jason's death, but I didn't want to hear any more of his lies."

Brittany wasn't all the way sold that Clarence would actually cheat on Ashley.

"But what if that's actually the truth?"

Ashley was shocked that she seemed to take his side. It showed in her facial expression.

"What if he didn't sleep with the woman? I mean, I know it sounds crazy because of what she said when she answered the phone but I mean you never know"

Ashley was so irritated at the moment. She no longer wanted to talk about the situation.

"I don't even care anymore Brittany"

She got up from the bed and went into the bathroom. She turned on the shower and began to get undressed. Brittany went back into the living room and laid down. After showering and getting dressed Ashley walked into the living room.

"I'll be back, Brittany." Brittany sat up.

"Where are you going, Ashley?"

"I need to go get some information." She headed towards the door and Brittany yelled out to her.

"Do you need me to go with you?" Ashley didn't respond as she walked out of the apartment.

About thirty minutes later Ashley pulled up to Mr. Rich's bar. She climbed out of the car and walked inside. She took her sunglasses off and made her way to the bar. Mr. Rich was behind the bar cleaning.

"Umm, hello." Ashley called out to him. Mr. Rich turned around slowly.

"Hey there, lady." There was a big smile on his face.

"How you been and how's the baby?"

"We're both fine Mr. Rich, but I'm here because I need to talk with your new bartender."

Mr. Rich pointed to a woman who was sitting at a table alone.

"That's her right over there, ma'am."

"Ok thanks, Mr. Rich, its good seeing you again." He smiled and nodded his head as he watched her walk over to Karen. Ashley reached the table and asked the woman if she could sit down.

"My name is Ashley."

"Hello, Ashley, I'm Karen. How may I help you?" Karen smiled as Ashley sat down in front of her.

"Well, I know you don't know me, but I think you know my boyfriend, Clarence"

Karen had a glass of orange juice which she took a sip from before she responded to Ashley.

"Oh you're Clarence's girlfriend; he told me so much about you."

"Ok I don't really care to hear what he told you about me, but the fact that he told you things about me lets me know that you knew about me, so why would you sleep with him knowing he had a girlfriend at home?"

211

Karen snickered after hearing her accusation. Though Ashley wasn't amused at all.

"Ashley, we didn't sleep with each other, sweetheart." Ashley wasn't buying it.

"But when he called your phone you said 'I'm still in the same position you left me in.'" Again, she laughed a little.

"I was only joking; me and Clarence didn't have sex at all." Ashley stared at her trying to read right through her, but she couldn't tell whether or not if Karen was lying.

"Listen, Ashley, we had a few drinks, and things got out of hand, and as a woman, I'm apologizing to you it should have never even gotten that far. But I assure you that nothing happened between us."

Ashley sat still with a confused look on her face. She had no idea what to believe. Being pregnant didn't help the cause either because her emotions were all over the place.

"Clarence is a good man, Ashley. I mean, not too many men would have done what he did. I mean, he left, and I could tell that he really didn't want to cheat on you."

Ashley was just upset that he would even put himself in that position.

"Clarence told me that you seem to know something about Jason's death."

Karen's smile quickly disappeared.

"Well, I don't know much about his death, but I do know about some guy who has been looking for him."

The two of them sat and talked for another forty five minutes. Ashley eventually wound up leaving the bar, and she headed to Clarence's apartment. She didn't even call to let him know that she was coming. As she made her way to the door, she took her time before she knocked. After a few knocks, Clarence opened the door.

"Hey, Ashley, what are you doing here?"

"Clarence, can I please come in? We really need to talk." He let her in with no hesitation.

"Clarence, I went to the bar and talked to Karen."

"Oh, God, Ashley, why would you do that?" Ashley made her way to the sofa.

"Clarence, that's not why I came over here." Clarence didn't sit down right away he stood at the edge of the sofa.

"I've been keeping something from you, Clarence." Hearing her say that bothered Clarence, so he sat next to her.

"What is it Ashley?" She took a deep breath and then exhaled.

"Remember when I told you I went to the doctor the other day?" She paused.

"Ashley, what is it?" Tears slowly began to fall from her face.

"Clarence, the doctor felt lumps on my breast."

"What are you saying, Ashley?" A tear dropped from his eye.

"Clarence, the doctor found signs of cancer"

28

"What do you mean signs of cancer?"

Clarence's voice began to crack. He turned his head to wipe his eyes because he didn't want Ashley to see the tears falling.

"Clarence, listen to me." She moved closer to him and put her hand on his leg.

"He said there are signs, and if I do happen to have cancer, we'll be able to catch it early which will give us a chance to treat it and hopefully cure it."

Clarence stood up and walked into his bedroom. Ashley didn't follow him. She stayed on the sofa. Surprisingly, she didn't begin to cry. She actually was able to maintain her composure. Ashley was able to handle it better than Clarence. Clarence made his way back into the living room and sat next to her.

"I can't believe all this is happening at once, it's like we're going through hell." He sat staring at the floor.

"Things aren't supposed to be like this. I mean, we're having a baby, it's supposed to be a beautiful experience, but I can't seem to find any reason to smile."

Ashley stared at him as he spoke. She was still upset with what happened between him and Melinda, so she chose to keep quiet until she could find the right words to say.

"I feel like this is all my fault, Ashley."

"How could this be your fault, Clarence, it's a part of life, but we can't sit here and point fingers or question why; all we can do is stay strong and get through it."

When she finally spoke, the tone of her voice, which actually remained calm, caused Clarence to raise his head and look her in her eyes.

"But, Ashley, I haven't made things any easier for you. I mean, the whole Jason situation, and then with the woman the other night. I've caused so much stress to you." He could see in Ashley's facial expression that she wasn't really interested in what he was saying. She tried to hide it but she was unsuccessful.

"Clarence, I don't really want to talk about all of that right now. I didn't come over here for that, I just came to tell you what the doctor told me and that's pretty much it."

She grabbed her purse and keys and stood up.

"I'm sorry; Clarence, but I can't do this right now." Clarence stood to his feet.

"What are you talking about, Ashley?"

"This whole act that you're putting on. I mean, every time something happens, you disappear and when I catch up with you there's always another woman around, so what are you going to do now that I've told you I may have cancer?" Clarence had no answer for her. He was lost and it showed in his face.

"Yeah, Clarence, exactly; you have nothing to say, so go ahead and run to one of them, and try that sad role with them and maybe they'll believe you, but I won't do it anymore. I've put up with these lies for too long; you don't love me, Clarence, you love yourself and I think it's time you take a look in the mirror and grow up." She turned and walked towards the door. Clarence ran behind her.

"Ashley, wait." She stopped just before she made it to the front door.

"You know that I love you more than anything, and I know I've messed up, but none of those women mean anything to me. I don't know why I even had them around. I've been going through so much and I just..." He paused in mid-sentence because he really didn't know what to say.

"Clarence, you didn't need to run to them when everything seemed to go wrong. You could've come to me that's how relationships work, but you didn't care, you obviously didn't know who was really there for you and who wasn't and now look at what you have to deal with."

Clarence stood in front of her speechless.

"Funny thing, Clarence, is every time after you went to them and things didn't go the way you planned, you always came running back to me and I embraced you with open arms, but you took that for granted and now it's all blowing up in your face."

She opened the door.

"I have a doctor's appointment in a couple days; I'll call you and let you know about the results." She began to walk outside.

"ASHLEY, WAIT."

Clarence screamed out. It was too late. She closed the door and walked away. Clarence turned and made his way back to the sofa and began to talk to himself.

"I can't believe this is all happening to me. I mean, where the hell did I go wrong?"

He knew he couldn't sit in his apartment alone because there was too much on his mind. In the past whenever things would get tough, he would just call on Jason. Now that Jason was no longer around, he could only depend on one person to give it to him straight and that was Mr. Rich. So, he jumped up and got dressed then headed to his bar. When he walked in, he saw the usual faces. Mr. Rich's bar seemed to have the same customers every day. Mostly middle-aged men who would come after a long day's work. Most of them construction workers. Every now and then there would be a group of women who would come in for a mid-day drink. He caught Mr. Rich as he was walking from the back. He approached the bar slowly.

"Hey, Clarence, you here to take home my bartender again?" He laughed loudly. Clarence barely cracked a smile.

"Mr. Rich, do you have a minute or two?"

Mr. Rich saw the seriousness in his eyes, so he walked from behind the bar.

"Sure thing, Clarence, let's go sit down somewhere and talk." He led Clarence to a table sitting in a corner in the back of the bar.

"What's going on, son?" Mr. Rich asked as they both began to sit down.

217

"Mr. Rich, I'm really going through it, man. I don't even know where to begin."

"Begin with whatever is bothering you the most." Clarence paused for about a minute to gather his thoughts.

"I fucked up bad, Mr. Rich, I really feel like I'm losing Ashley."

"First off, son, let me tell you this; you put yourself into this situation, and I don't even know why because you're not that kind of guy." Clarence had no idea what Mr. Rich was talking about and Mr. Rich could tell.

"By that I mean, you tried to step outside of your zone you took Karen home, and you tried to get you some on the side; that's not your character, son, so that's why you got caught up."

"Mr. Rich how do you know that I got caught?" His response made Mr. Rich smile.

"Son, you've been knowing me all this time, you should know by now that nothing gets past Mr. Rich's eyes." Clarence shook his head.

"You see, Clarence, that's the problem with you young boys, y'all try and do things that are outside of y'all nature and then get mad when it doesn't work for y'all, then try to blame someone else for the shit that comes along with it." He reached into his shirt pocket and pulled out a cigarette.

"What I'm saying, Clarence is that you're not the player type; you're a one woman kind of man, so stick to that. I mean, you had yourself a pretty good woman who seems to love you, and you messed that up for what?" He lit the cigarette and took a few puffs.

"Now, don't get me wrong, I know Karen is tough and she's hard to resist, but the type of guy that you are, you have to or else it's not going to work for you."

"But, Mr. Rich, you've been married for as long as I can remember, and you always step outside of home." Mr. Rich laughed so hard it made him choke on the cigarette smoke.

"But that's because I'm built for that; you and me are two different breeds, son. Don't get me wrong, I love my wife but the reason I've never been caught is because I'm built for that type of lifestyle. When God created me, it's almost like he gave me super powers. I can make a woman disappear so quick, my wife will never get a chance to see what I have going on." That brought a smile to Clarence's face.

"There are two types of guy's in this world, Clarence." He put his cigarette out.

"There's the lovers and the likers" He looked Clarence in his eyes.

"The lovers, which you seem to be, are the type of guys that would do anything for their woman, the type of guy that will put his jacket down to cover a puddle, so she won't get her new shoes wet. Now, a liker like myself would tell her either to jump over it or get her feet wet; now, don't get things confused, yes I am married and I love my wife, but outside of that, any other woman I just like."

"Mr. Rich, you sure have a weird way of explaining things, but I think I understand where you're coming from" They both laughed.

"So, what else is bothering you, son?"

"Well, of course the whole situation with Jason, of course." Mr. Rich grabbed his cigarette and lit it up again.

"Clarence, this is a bad situation, son. The cops have been all over my place; they really want you bad. I mean, they're saying you killed the guy." Clarence tried to speak, but Mr. Rich didn't give him a chance.

"Now, I don't have no proof that can really help you, but you know Mr. Rich always finds things out, and I think I know who killed your friend."

Just as Mr. Rich began to give Clarence his thoughts on what happened to Jason, he paused because he saw Karen coming towards the table out the corner of his eye.

"Mr. Rich, your wife is on the telephone." He put down his cigarette.

"Tell her I'm busy, won't ya, sweetheart?"

"I tried to, but she kept saying it's an emergency." He dropped his head and let out a deep sigh.

"Ok, I'm coming." He stood up from his chair and grabbed his cigarette.

"But, Mr. Rich, you haven't finished telling me what happened." Mr. Rich held out his hand asking Clarence to give him a moment.

"I'll be right back, son."

He walked off to answer the phone. Karen stood in front of the table instead of heading back to the bar with Mr. Rich. She and Clarence both stared each other down.

"So, what's going on Clarence?" Karen asked awkwardly.

"Umm, same ole, same ole I guess," Clarence responded while looking at the table. For some reason, he couldn't answer her and look her in the eyes at the same time.

"Do you mind if I sit down for a second?" He shrugged his shoulders.

"It's a free country, isn't it?"

She pulled out the chair that Mr. Rich had been sitting in and sat down. Clarence began to tap his fingers on the table and look around the bar.

"Clarence, what's wrong?" He stopped tapping the table and looked at her.

"What did you tell Ashley?" Karen smiled.

"Clarence calm down, I didn't tell her anything."

Clarence began to tap his fingers on the table again. His frustration was beginning to build. In his mind, he felt like Karen must have told Ashley something because of the how Ashley just up and left him.

"You're lying, Karen, you had to tell her something because she told me she was done and she left me." Karen smiled again.

"You think that's funny, Karen, you messed everything up between me and her."

"Now, you wait just a minute, Clarence, it was your idea to come to my house. You're a grown man; you made that decision knowing you had a girlfriend who happens to be pregnant waiting at home for you, so don't blame that on me."

By this time Karen was the one tapping her fingers on the table. The frustration had shifted.

"But you said you knew that I had a girlfriend, so how do I know that you weren't trying to set me up or something?" Her jaw dropped.

"Clarence, let's be serious for a second, I'm a grown single woman and I have my needs. You seemed available at the time, so I felt like taking care of my needs. Now, it wasn't right and I even expressed that to Ashley, but it is what it is nothing happened between us, so that's over but that's not even what I wanted to talk to you about." Mr. Rich made his way back to the table. He had his jacket on and keys in his hand.

"Karen, baby, I gotta go handle some business at home. Clarence, you and me will finish talking, son. I'll give you a call later." Clarence jumped out of his chair.

"Mr Rich wait"

"Clarence its important don't worry we'll talk" He hurried out of the bar and Clarence sat back down.

"DAMN!"

He screamed out and slammed his fist down on the table.

"Clarence, remember the guy I told you that's been coming in here looking for you?" Clarence looked at her and nodded his head.

"Well, he normally comes around this time, and I have a feeling he's on his way, so maybe you should leave."

"No, I'm not going anywhere. If somebody wants to talk to me, then we can sit down like men and talk." Karen stood up and shrugged her shoulders.

"Ok, well, I need to get back to the bar, Clarence, do you need anything?" He shook his head.

"If the guy comes in here, I'll be sure to send him your way."

"Yeah, do that, please."

Karen walked back to the bar. Clarence sat at the bar playing with his phone for about twenty minutes, and just as Karen called it, the man who had been checking for Clarence entered the bar. He spoke with Karen for a few minutes, and she pointed him in Clarence's direction. The man walked up to Clarence, but he had his head down so he had no idea there was someone standing over him.

"Excuse me, sir, do you mind if I have a few minutes of your time?"

Clarence looked up and it was John. Definitely not the person Clarence wanted to see. He jumped up and was ready for a fight. John held out his arms and tried to calm him down.

"Hold on buddy let's not get ahead of ourselves I didn't come here for that. I'm here to try and help you." He pulled out a chair and sat down. Clarence was still standing as he watched him take a seat.

"Are you going to stay on your feet the whole time or are you going to sit down" Clarence was breathing hard and his heart was racing. He decided to hear him out and he took a seat.

"Now, Clarence, I've spoke to a lot of people, and they're all telling me that you and Jason had a first fight the night he was killed."

"That's bullshit." Clarence screamed out.

"Well, be that as it may, Clarence, there are plenty of people saying otherwise. Now, what I'm here to tell you is I have a friend who is a great lawyer, and he may be able to get this thing down to maybe self-defense, and the charges won't be as serious."

Clarence stared John in his eyes as he spoke. There was something about the man that just didn't sit right with him. He didn't trust John at all.

"Why are you trying to help me out?" John smirked at Clarence.

"Well, as you know, I know your girlfriend very well, and let's just say I owe her one."

After hearing that, Clarence, became even more upset. He jumped from his seat again. This time, he got into John's face.

"You listen to me, John; I want you to stay away from Ashley."

John laughed. It was obvious he didn't take Clarence serious at all.

"Or what, Clarence, you gonna kill me like you killed Jason?"

John stood to his feet, and they were both standing face to face.

"And then what, you gonna go to jail for two murders, and you'll never be able to spend time with your kid. You better think twice on how you speak to me, boy, or else."

He bumped Clarence and began to walk off. John turned to Clarence and said,

"You know what, you can forget about me helping you out. I wouldn't mind spending time with Ashley and the baby anyways, I mean someone has to take care of home."

He smiled and walked away.

Clarence went back and sat at the table. His mind was all over the place. His girlfriend was pregnant with his child, and she just got word that she may have cancer. On top of that, his best friend was killed and all fingers were pointing at him. He wanted to put his hands on John, but that would've only made matters worse. Karen walked to the table and sat down. She had a concerned look on her face. She watched the encounter between John and Clarence from behind the bar.

"Clarence, are you ok?" Clarence didn't even look at her. His mind was so far gone.

"Why didn't you tell me that the man who was looking for me was John" He had his hands crossed on the table. He asked her the question but still didn't make eye contact with her.

"John is that his name" Clarence looked at her as if she was holding back information or acting clueless.

"Clarence, I told you I didn't know his name. Hell, I've never really had a real conversation with him. Every time he comes in here, he asks for you." To say that Clarence was frustrated would be an understatement. It definitely began to show.

"What exactly did he ask, Karen?"

"Clarence, he would come in here and ask when was the last time you came in or how long did you stay the last time you came in—things like that." Clarence shook his head.

"But at the time, I didn't really know how to respond because I wasn't sure what was going on." Clarence pulled out his cell phone and scrolled through his contacts and made a call. There was no answer, so he put the phone on the table.

"Clarence, I don't really know what's going on, but I'd really like to help you." He just stared at her while she spoke.

"Please, tell me how you can help me, Karen. I mean, people are saying I killed my best friend, my girlfriend is pregnant and wants nothing to do with me, and she…" He stopped before he said too much. His eyes began to water, but none of the tears fell. Karen could see the hurt in his eyes but she wasn't sure what to say.

"Clarence, I'm not really sure what to say. I wish there was more I can do." She stood up and placed her hand on his shoulder.

"I have to get back to the bar, but if you need anything, just let me know." She headed back to the bar. Clarence didn't stay much longer after she walked away. While he was sitting at the table, he called Ashley but she didn't answer. After he got into his car he called her again. No answer. So, he then called Mr. Rich. He didn't pick up either. Clarence decided to just drive to Ashley's apartment. He figured he could try and talk to her and smooth things out. He made it to her apartment and quickly found a parking spot. He ran up the stairs and began to knock on her door. Brittany was the one to open it.

"Ashley isn't here, Clarence." She began to close the door but Clarence stopped her.

"Wait, Brittany." She pulled the door back open.

"What is it, Clarence, you're making me miss my show." "I need to talk to you." Brittany wasn't too sure what to say to Clarence at the moment, so she began to close the door. Again, he stopped her.

"Please," He begged her. She then opened the door and allowed him to walk inside. They both made their way into the living room. Brittany sat on the sofa, and Clarence sat on the love seat.

"So, what is there to talk about, Clarence?"

"Where is Ashley?" Brittany smiled.

"I don't know, Clarence." She pulled out her phone and began to play around with it.

"What do you mean you don't know?"

"Clarence, I don't keep her in my back pocket. I don't keep tabs on her. I mean maybe she went to the doctor. I don't know." Her response was so sarcastic it bothered Clarence.

"Why do you have to say it like that, Brittany?"

"Say it like what, Clarence?" He shrugged his shoulders.

"I don't know, it seems like you have an attitude."

"I really don't know what you expect me to say right now, Clarence. I mean, I was actually in your corner for a while, but you changed and you really hurt Ashley. You know that she's my best friend, and I just lost all respect for you."

Clarence was speechless. He wasn't expecting to hear those words from Brittany.

"When you were out doing only God knows what, I was the one taking care of her, I was the one going with her on her doctor visits, I was here to wipe her tears, Clarence, and where were you?"

By this time, Brittany had become disgusted just from looking at Clarence's face. The two of them never really had the opportunity to sit and have a one on one.

"I didn't know what to do, Brittany, there was just so much going on."

"That's bullshit, Clarence!" She yelled out. Brittany put her phone on the coffee table.

"You don't just leave the mother of your child alone when things get hard. I mean, are you a man or what?"

Clarence stood up.

"Yeah, what you gonna do now, huh, you just gonna run out again like you did to her?"

"YOU DON'T KNOW WHAT THE HELL I'VE BEEN DEALING WITH, BRITTANY!" The tone of his voice changed. This was the first time Brittany saw this side of Clarence.

"Having to deal with everything that was going on with Ashley and not to mention Jason, that's tough. I mean, I never wanted things to turn out this way. I just didn't know what to do. And now to find out that she has cancer just makes things even more difficult to deal with." Brittany's jaw dropped to the floor.

"Cancer" She had no idea because Ashley had yet to break the news to her.

"What are you talking about, Clarence?"

Clarence sat back down on the love seat. Meanwhile, Mr. Rich had made it home. He walked into his two story house to see his wife sitting in the living room. His wife stood at about five foot three and had long gray hair. Her age showed in her hair but not in her face. For a woman her age, there was not a wrinkle in sight. Not on her face at least.

"Hey, baby, what's wrong?" She looked at him with a face full of fear.

"Harold, tell me what's going on."

Harold happened to be his government name. Mr. Rich was just a nickname that was given to him from his old buddies from back in the day. He was a big time gambler, so it pretty much came from that.

"What are you talking about, sweetheart, tell me what's wrong."

"Harold, some man came by here looking for you, and he was very aggressive." Mr. Richs' smirk turned into a frown within a matter of seconds.

"Harold, I'm worried." she stood up and placed her hands on his face.

"This isn't one of those guys from your past is it?" He shook his head.

"Are you sure, Harold; you don't owe anybody any money, do you? If so, we have plenty saved up, and we can pay it off, or I can call my brother to help us out if we don't have enough. Please, Harold, just tell me what's going on."

"Teresa, calm down, baby, everything is going to be just fine" He grabbed her hands and kissed them both.

"Just tell me what else did he say to you?" Her hands began to shake as he held onto them.

"Well, he just asked what time would you be back and if you were down at the bar." She was so nervous; sweat began to form on her forehead.

"I told him I wasn't sure, and then he said to give you a call and that he'd hate for you to end up like your friend. Harold, what is he talking about?"

229

She was so anxious; her words were coming out her mouth so fast Mr. Rich could barely keep up. Then, there was a knock at the door that caused them both to jump. Teresa's heart dropped.

"Let me get the door, sweetheart."

Mr. Rich let go of her hands and walked towards the door. He took a deep breath before he opened it. Teresa watched nervously as he opened up the door. It was the same man that had come by earlier and spoke to her. She couldn't hear what Mr. Rich said to him, but he let him inside. The two men walked towards Teresa. The man flashed a grin at her.

"Nice to see you again, ma'am. He said to her as his smile widened.

"Umm, Teresa, can you give us a few minutes alone?" Mr. Rich asked his wife.

"Sure, Harold, I'll be in the kitchen."

She turned and walked to the kitchen. As she walked off, she looked back a few times and saw both guys waiting for her to disappear. After she made it to the kitchen, they both sat down. Mr. Rich stared at the man and his displeasure was evident.

"What the hell are you doing here?" He tried his best to keep his voice quiet so that Teresa wouldn't hear him.

"You and me have business to tend to, sir," The man replied.

"John, first off, let me ask you what the hell are you doing here? How dare you show up to my house, showing up to my job is already beginning to piss me off, and you pull this shit."

John sat in front of Mr. Rich with a big smile on his face. Which seemed to upset Mr. Rich even more.

"Then, you have the nerve to sit there with that stupid smile on your face. I should kick your ass."

John's smile disappeared. He reached into his pants and pulled out a gun and sat it on the coffee table.

"Now, Mr. Rich, why would you want to do something like that? I thought we were supposed to be friends?" The sarcasm irked Mr. Rich.

"Now, you know damn..."

Mr. Rich paused when he saw John reaching for the gun. John pulled his hand back once Mr. Rich stopped talking.

"What's up with all the hostility, sir? I just came over here to say hello, I don't want any trouble."

"What the hell you mean you don't want any trouble? You pop up at my house, and then you pull a gun out. I should call the police on your ass."

John then grabbed the gun and sat it on his lap.

"Now, why would you want to do that, Mr. Rich? I mean, you do know I know about your little gambling habit and all of the illegal activity you have going on down there at that little bar of yours. I'm sure you don't want them showing up to your little establishment and I have a few friends down at the precinct, so all it takes is one phone call."

Mr. Rich closed his eyes and took a deep breath. He opened his eyes and stared at John while trying to choose the right words to say.

"Ok, John, what's the real reason you're here?"

"I told you, Mr. Rich, I just wanted to say hello." Again, he flashed an evil grin at Mr. Rich.

"Oh yeah, and umm, I just wanted to make sure we still had our little agreement intact. I mean, I haven't seen you in a while, and I would hope that you weren't trying to back out of it." He still had his hand on his gun and Mr. Rich watched his every move.

"Speaking of that little bar of yours, I went down there today, and I saw your little friend, Clarence." Mr. Rich looked him into his eyes, and the disgust showed all in his face.

"Poor guy, Mr. Rich, he seems to have a lot on his mind, and it's such a shame what happened to that friend of his. I mean, murdering a guy over a woman is such a poor decision, you know. I once had a guy who didn't like me because of a woman, but it never really bothered me much because I knew there was no way that he could take her from me, even if me and her went our separate ways, I still would be able to have her anytime I wanted."

Mr. Rich was confused as to why John was making that confession.

"But that's another story for another day, sir, now let me ask you again."

He picked the gun up and held it on his knee and pointed it at Mr. Rich.

"Are you still going to hold up on your side of the agreement that we made or are we going to have to take an alternative route?"

Mr. Rich's wife walked back into the living room. John had his back towards her, so she couldn't see him holding the gun. As he heard her approaching he put the gun back into his pants. Both John and Mr. Rich jumped up.

"Hey, baby, I was just going to cook. I wanted to know if you and your friend were hungry."

She had a feeling that something was wrong, so she made up something quick to try and be nosey.

"Oh no, sweetheart, he's actually about to leave."

Mr. Rich nervously looked into Johns eyes. John smiled.

"Are you sure, I mean you can't just come to a person's house and not eat a little something. Plus, you look like you haven't had a good meal in days."

"Teresa, its fine. Umm, he was just here trying to tell me about some kinda insurance for the bar, but I told him we're already covered." Teresa could tell there was more to it than just some insurance talk, but she gave in.

"Yeah, ma'am, he's right I do have to get going. I have a few other clients I have to go and speak with, but thank you anyway. Next time I'm around, I'll come by so I can get some of that good home cooking." He headed towards the door and Mr. Rich followed.

"Teresa, I'm going to walk him to his car. I'll be right back."

They both walked outside, and Mr. Rich closed the door behind them. Teresa ran over to the window to look and see what was going on. Outside, Mr. Rich and John walked to John's car.

"I like how you covered that up, Mr. Rich. I see you're quick on your toes, so that leads me to believe that you know how to keep your mouth shut." He smiled at Mr. Rich and opened his car door. Before he got in he had a few last words for Mr. Rich.

"You make sure you tell our little friend, Clarence, there's nothing he can do now, and he's just going to have to suffer the consequences."

He smiled and then got into his car. Mr. Rich tapped his window before he started the engine. John rolled his window down and then lit up a cigarette.

"Don't you ever come by my house again, and you leave Clarence alone."

John took a few puffs from his cigarette and then blew the smoke into Mr. Rich's face. He started the car and then drove off. Mr. Rich stormed back into the house. Teresa jumped from the window to try and act as if she wasn't watching.

"Is everything ok, Harold?" He didn't want to worry her any more than she already was, so he played it cool.

"Yeah, baby, everything is fine. You know those insurance guys can be so pushy at times, but he was only doing his job."

He walked away from her and into the kitchen. Mr. Rich then pulled out his cell phone and called Clarence. Clarence was still at Ashley's apartment talking to Brittany. Brittany's eyes began to water just as she heard the news about Ashley's cancer. Clarence heard his phone ring, so he reached into his pocket and pulled it out. He saw that it was Mr. Rich calling, so he immediately answered.

"Clarence, I need you to drop whatever it is you're doing and meet me at the bar now."

"Ok, Mr. Rich, but what's wrong?" Mr. Rich had already hung up. Clarence put the phone back into his pocket and stood up.

"Look, Brittany, I have to go, but look, I'll be back. So, tell Ashley ok?"

It was almost like Brittany didn't hear a word he said. She just stared at the wall. Clarence walked up to her and put his hand on her shoulder.

"Look, I know it's tough, but things will get better; don't worry."

She still had nothing to say. Clarence ran to the door. As soon as he opened the door, there was Ashley on the other side reaching into her purse for her keys. She looked up when she heard the door open. Clarence froze once he saw that it was her. Neither one of them knew what to say.

"Clarence, what are you doing here?" She asked him as she made her way into the apartment.

"And how did..."

She paused once she looked into the living room and saw Brittany sitting on the sofa. Ashley turned and looked at Clarence with an upset look on her face.

"Ashley, don't even get the wrong idea. It's not what you think, I swear." She shook her head and walked towards Brittany, who had begun to cry on the sofa.

"Brittany, why did you let him in? I thought we talked about this." She didn't notice that Brittany was crying because she turned, so she couldn't see her face.

"BRITTANY!" Ashley yelled to try and get her attention. Brittany slowly turned her head, and her eyes were full of tears.

"What's wrong, Brittany?" She sat next to her on the sofa.

"Clarence, what did you do to her?" Clarence held his hands in the air.

"I didn't do anything, Ashley"

"Ashley, why didn't you tell me?" She wiped the tears that began falling down her cheeks.

"Tell you what Brittany, What's going on here"

"Why didn't you tell me you have cancer?"

Brittany's voice cracked as she tried to hold back her anger. Ashley's jaw dropped. She looked down at the floor and then turned her attention back to Clarence. Before she said anything, she stared him down. Clarence closed his eyes and took a deep breath. He knew that Ashley was going to let him have it. Only thing is, she didn't. She turned her attention back to Brittany.

"Brittany, I was going to tell you when I knew for sure. I didn't want to scare you."

"Ashley, I'm your best friend. I should have been the first one you told. I mean, how could you tell this good for nothing son of a..."

"Brittany, stop it."

"No, you stop it, Ashley. I mean, he's never around, and he's put you through so much bullshit. I can't believe he knew and I didn't."

"Of course he knows, Brittany. I am pregnant with his child."

Brittany stood up and walked into the kitchen. Clarence stood in silence. His phone began to ring again. He pulled it out to see it was Mr. Rich. He let the phone ring and put it back into his pocket.

"Look, Brittany, I don't want any static between the two of us." She didn't pay any attention to him. He walked up to Ashley.

"Look, Ashley, I have to go take care of some business." She sucked her teeth and folded her arms across her chest.

"You see what I'm talking about, Ashley, he's good for nothing, and this is the man you chose to have a baby with."

Ashley held her out to try and get Brittany to stop before she said something she would regret.

"Brittany, please don't be disrespectful. I know you're upset with me right now, but please, just watch what you say."

Brittany stood still and shook her head. She was really upset. Mainly because of the sickness her friend was dealing with. Not only that, she couldn't stand the sight of Clarence.

"Ok, whatever, Ashley. Look, I can't stand to be in the same room with this guy here, so as long as he's going to be here, I'm going elsewhere." She stormed out of the apartment. Ashley chased after her.

"BRITTANY, WAIT!" She yelled out, but Brittany didn't stop. She continued to walk to the parking lot. Ashley walked back into the apartment. She was out of breath and began to cough. Clarence ran to her and grabbed her by the arm.

"Ashley, are you ok?" She nodded her head.

"I'm fine Clarence I just need to lay down" She went into her bedroom and laid across the bed. Clarence walked in behind her and stood at the foot of the bed.

"Ashley, I'm sorry for everything I've been putting you through, but I was wondering if we could—" Before he could finish, her loud coughs caused him to stop in mid-sentence.

"Clarence, can you go into the kitchen and get me a bottle of water out the fridge?"

He nodded his head and walked into the kitchen. Clarence returned with a bottle of water. Ashley's eyes were closed.

"Ashley." her eyes didn't open when he called her name.

"Ashley," he called out again, and she still didn't open her eyes. He sat on the bed next to her and began to rub his fingers through her hair. Her eyes slowly opened.

"Clarence."

"Yes, Ashley?"

"I don't want to die." Those words hit Clarence right in the heart. He didn't know what to say. Ashley began to cry, and that made him feel even worse.

"You're not going to die, baby, we're going to get through this."

"What do you mean 'we're'?"

"I mean, I'm going to be right by your side through all of this, and there's no way you can die. We are gonna have our baby and have our own little family."

Ashley tried to crack a smile, but her chest pains wouldn't allow her to do so.

"I just want to go to sleep, Clarence." He leaned down and kissed her forehead and then whispered in her ear,

"I love you."

Ashley turned over and closed her eyes. Clarence left her apartment and headed to meet up with Mr. Rich. As soon as he walked into the bar, Mr. Rich walked up to him. He didn't even say a word he grabbed him by the arm and walked to a table in the back of the bar where they could sit and talk alone.

"What took you so long to get here, Clarence, I've been calling your phone."

Mr. Rich seemed to be very nervous. He began twitching his fingers. He even bit his nails a few times.

"Mr. Rich, calm down and tell me what's going on."

"It's that son of a bitch, John." Clarence had grown tired of hearing that man's name. His stomach would turn just at the thought of him.

"Ok, what now?" he replied with disgust.

"He's a damn lunatic; he showed up at my house today and even had a gun on him." Clarence stared at Mr. Rich with his mouth wide open.

"My wife was there, Clarence, and I had to lie to her now you know how much I hate lying to my wife."

"Mr. Rich, that's all you do, is lie to your wife," Clarence snickered.

"I don't lie to her, boy, I tell the half the truth, and that's only when I'm training my new bartenders, but that's not the point I'm trying to make, boy. I'm telling you, this guy is after you, and he wants you to go down. What exactly did you do to this man to make him so upset with you?"

Clarence shrugged his shoulders.

"Mr. Rich, I have no idea. I mean, first, he started off acting like he was cool, and then just out the blue, he changed up."

"Isn't he your old lady's ex?" Clarence nodded his head.

"Well, there it is, son, he's jealous you took his lady and knocked her up." Mr. Rich shook his head.

"See, that's the problem with you young cats these days, y'all are so emotional when it comes to these women out here. I just don't understand it." Clarence had no response.

"Oh y'all, don't want the woman and wanna treat her like a pile of cat shit, and then get mad when another man comes around and puts a smile on her face; that's a damn shame."

He pulled out a pack of cigarettes. He shook the pack until the last cigarette fell onto the table.

"Me and my wife been married for years, and the only man to put on her face besides me is Jesus. Well, him and the doctor when he told her she wasn't pregnant, but that was a long time ago." Clarence tried his best not to laugh, but he couldn't help it.

"Don't laugh, boy, this is a serious time. What are you going to do about this fella?"

"Mr. Rich, what am I supposed to do? I mean, if he wants to get me, then he can come and get me, but I won't go down without a fight. I guarantee you that."

Mr. Rich lit his cigarette and began to smoke. The smoke blew into Clarence's face and he waved his hands to clear the air. Once the smoke disappeared, he looked to the front door and saw someone walk in that he did not want to run into. It was Brittany. She walked to the bar and spoke to Karen who was behind the bar making drinks for a few customers. Karen pointed her to an empty table, and she walked over and sat down. Clarence kept his eyes on her from the minute she walked in till the minute she sat down. He watched her for a few minutes, and Mr. Rich continued to smoke his cigarette. What happened next though was the icing on the cake. There was a man who walked in wearing a long trench coat and a baseball cap. The cap was pulled over his eyes, but Clarence had an idea who it was. He recognized the man's walk. The man walked to the bar just as Brittany did just minutes earlier. And he was also directed to the same table as her. He made his way to the table. Brittany stood up and gave the man a hug. The man then gave her a kiss on the cheek. Clarence couldn't believe his eyes.

"CLARENCE!" Mr. Rich yelled out but Clarence was stuck. He couldn't even hear him calling. He just stared at the man and Brittany as they sat and talked.

29

"Clarence, what's wrong?"

Mr. Rich asked Clarence who was still staring in Brittany's direction. Mr. Rich turned around to see what Clarence was staring at. He then turned back and looked Clarence in his eyes.

"Oh no, Clarence, I'm going to the back, and I'm going to shoot that son of a..."

Clarence pulled Mr. Rich back down to his seat as he was trying to jump up and head to the back.

"Wait, Mr. Rich, don't do that; let's just wait a few minutes. Don't cause a scene."

"What the hell do you mean wait, Clarence? I can't let this guy think that he can just do whatever he wants, I'm tired of it."

Mr. Rich began breathing so hard it seemed as if he was going to have a heart attack. But in true Mr. Rich fashion, he pulled out his pack of cigarettes and lit one up. He had been smoking cigarettes since he was a teenager. It was pretty much his stress reliever.

"Mr. Rich, look, I know you're pissed, hell, I'm pissed too. But let's not make things worse than they already are. Like I said, let's wait a few minutes, and I'll go over there and handle it myself."

Mr. Rich gave Clarence a side eye and continued to smoke his cigarette. The man didn't even stay long. Maybe about five minutes. He pulled out what looked to be a card and gave it to Brittany. He then stood up from the table and walked outside the bar. Mr. Rich felt his cell phone vibrate in his pants. He pulled the phone out and answered it.

"Hello."

"Don't think that I didn't see you sitting there at the table watching me, sir."

"What the hell do you want?"

"Oh nothing at all, sir, but I did see you sitting across from my good friend, Clarence, just make sure you tell him I said hello."

"I'm not telling him nothing, you asshole. Come back here and be a man, and you tell him yourself." The man on the other end of the phone had already hung up.

"Hello," Mr. Rich repeated three times in a row. He then threw his cell phone down on the floor, and the phone shattered everywhere.

"Mr. Rich, who was that?"

"I'm going to go over here to talk to this woman to straighten this shit out."

"Wait, Mr. Rich, let me go talk to her. It'll be better."

"Don't go over there trying to be friendly, Clarence, you get to the bottom of this, or I will, and it won't be pretty."

Clarence put his hand of Mr. Richs' shoulder then walked towards the table that Brittany was sitting at. She looked up and saw him coming and tried to put her head down, but it was already too late. She had already been spotted. Clarence pulled out a chair and sat down.

"What do you want, Clarence?"

"Are you really going to sit here and ask me what do I want?"

Clarence was furious, yet he remained calm. He didn't want to yell or anything that would bring attention to the two of them.

"Yes, I mean, what did you not understand what I said back at Ashley's apartment?"

"Listen, Brittany, I don't give a damn about what you said and how you feel towards my relationship with Ashley. That has nothing to do with you. Everything that happens between me and her is going to stay between me and her."

"Ok, so, like I said Clarence what exactly do you want?" The card that was given to her was sitting on the table, and Clarence had his eye on it. Once Brittany realized that he saw it, she tried to grab it, but she moved too slowly, and Clarence got his hands on it.

"So, what's this about, Brittany?"

"It's just a card, Clarence, damn. Now give it back, so I can go."

"What did he say to you? Did he mention my name?" Brittany didn't answer; she just shook her head and held her hand out. Clarence took the card and tore it up. Brittany rolled her eyes and sucked her teeth.

"Look, Clarence. I have to go, so since you obviously have nothing to talk about..."

"Tell me what he told you, Brittany."

"There's nothing for me to tell you, Clarence, all I can say to you is I hope you have a good lawyer." She stood up and grabbed her purse. "What the hell does that mean, Brittany?"

"Clarence, how could you put Ashley through all of this, and to think, at one point I had your back, and I thought you were the perfect man for her. But you're just like the rest of these scumbags out here. You want to play around out here like you don't have a woman sitting at home waiting on you, but don't worry, Clarence. Karma is one nasty bitch and she doesn't forget anybody. So, like I said, get you a lawyer, sir, because this could get ugly."

She walked away from him with a smirk on her face and walked out of the bar. Mr. Rich jumped up and walked over to Clarence.

"So, what did she say, Clarence?" he still had the same cigarette in his mouth, but it wasn't lit. Just hanging from his bottom lip. It almost looked as if the cigarette was attached to his lip.

"She told me I need to find myself a lawyer."

Mr. Rich looked around the bar and pulled out his pack of cigarettes. He opened the box and gave one to Clarence.

"Listen, son, let me take care of this situation. I can make all of these problems go away." Clarence lit his cigarette.

"Mr. Rich, I appreciate you for trying to help me out, but this is something I have to handle myself."

"Are you sure? Son, because all I have to do is make one phone call."

"Yes, Mr. Rich, I'm going to deal with it." He put his cigarette out on the table. A few ashes dropped to the floor, and Clarence kicked them away.

"I'm just going to lay low-key for a while and try and figure things out. I mean, I have a child on the way so that's my main focus"

"So, I guess I won't be seeing you around here for a while?"

"Yeah, Mr. Rich, it'll be a while before I come in here. I don't want to bring any more problems into your establishment; that's not fair to you."

"Oh, son, it's no big deal. You're like family. Whatever you go through, I'm going through it with you, but I respect and understand your decision. Just don't stay away too long." Clarence smiled.

"Mr. Rich, you have my number, feel free to call me anytime. This is just temporary. Everything will be ok; it's just best that I get things back on track."

Clarence held out his hand, but Mr. Rich went in for a hug. Mr. Rich was something like a father figure to Clarence, so even though Clarence told him that it was temporary it felt like a goodbye. The two of them hugged for a few minutes, and then Clarence made his way out of the bar.

30

Clarence left the bar with many questions unanswered. It was something he felt he needed to do. When he left the bar that day, he knew things were going to change. For the better, he hoped, but only time would tell. He drove to his apartment and sat in the car for about an hour just thinking to himself. After an hour, he pulled out his cell phone and got out of the car. He called Ashley, but there was no answer. Normally, he'd be worried when she wouldn't answer, but this time, it didn't really bother him. He walked inside of his apartment and sat on the sofa.

"How did my life become such a mess, Lord?" he said as he bowed his head and closed his eyes.

"Lord, I know that I have failed you. I've lost myself in this world, and I don't know how to get through everything that I'm dealing with. The only thing I know how to do is talk to you, Lord." Tears began rolling down his face as he continued to pray.

"Father, I trust that you will see me through, and I just want to thank you for bringing me this far. I just ask for guidance and strength, Lord, in Jesus name, I pray. AMEN."

He kept his eyes closed and laid across the sofa. Meanwhile, at Ashley's apartment, the reason she didn't answer the phone was because she was doing the same thing as Clarence. As soon as she finished praying, she heard a knock on the door. She opened the door and saw two men standing in suits. One of the men took off his sunglasses and pulled out his badge. He didn't even say a word. He just flashed his badge, and Ashley's heart dropped to the floor.

"Hello, ma'am, my name is Detective Adams, and this is my partner Detective Williams. We were wondering if we could come in and have a few words with you; maybe ask you a few questions?"

These were the same two men that had took Clarence in for questioning.

"Umm, I guess so."

Ashley responded as she slowly opened the door. She led both of them into the living room, and the two detectives sat down. Ashley didn't sit down.

"Would you two like anything to drink?"

"Yes, do you have any whiskey?"

Detective Williams answered with a grin on his face. Ashley frowned at him.

"Umm, no ma'am, we're ok." Detective Adams glared at his partner.

"We are here to ask you a few questions about your boyfriend, Mr. Clarence Robertson." She closed her eyes and took a deep breath.

"He is your boyfriend, isn't he?" Detective Williams asked with a sarcastic tone, still flashing that same grin.

"Uhh, what my partner means is you and Mr. Robertson have some sort of close relationship, correct?" Ashley nodded her head.

"Yes, he is my boyfriend, and the father of my child." Detective Williams snickered. Ashley looked at him.

"Is there something funny, sir?" She asked as she folded her arms across her chest.

"You have to excuse my partner." Detective Adams again tried to cover up for his partners antics.

"So, can you tell us, ma'am, when's the last time you heard from Clarence?"

"What do you guys want with Clarence?"

"We just want to know the last time you heard from him, that's all."

"I haven't talked to him in a couple days."

The two officers noticed that she didn't really feel comfortable talking about Clarence. At least not with them. She had an angry look on her face, and she began rubbing her stomach as she felt the baby kicking. Detective Williams sat and watched her every move.

"So, how far along are you, Miss Lady?"

"I thought you guys wanted to talk about Clarence?" he smiled at her.

"Ok, let's get right down to it; your boyfriend is the lead suspect in a murder case, and we need you to cooperate with us, so we can try and make life easier for you. Now if you work with us, then we can all benefit from it." Ashley shook her head.

"How the hell can I benefit from this? I'm six and a half months pregnant, and you're telling me that the father of my child is wanted for murder. I don't understand how I can benefit from this by working with the two of you." Detective Williams who was the more aggressive officer stood to his feet.

"Listen up here, you fat bit..." His partner jumped up and stood in front of him and cut him off before he could finish.

"Listen, from the information we have received, we were told that Clarence had a fight with the victim, and if you work with us, there's a chance that he can claim self-defense"

"I don't want to talk to you guys anymore." She walked towards the door and opened it.

"I would appreciate it if the two of you would just leave."

Both of the officers stood up and walked to the door. Detective Williams walked out first. He looked her in the eyes and laughed. Detective Adams followed, but stopped for a few more words.

"Listen, I know things are tough right now, but just think about what I told you. You have a child that's going to need both parents around, so consider it, and maybe we can get a deal done."

He reached into his jacket pocket and pulled out a card.

"Here's my card; give me a call if you change your mind." He held the card out, and Ashley hesitated before she took it. When she did take the card, she tore it up right in front of his face. He shook his head and walked off without saying another word. Ashley closed the door and stood against it. She began to cry. She heard her phone ringing from her bedroom, so she ran and grabbed it. It was Clarence.

"Hello, Clarence."

"Ashley, I love you," he responded.

"I love you too, Clarence but where are you? I need you to come over here; there are some things we need to talk about."

"Ok, Ashley, let me get myself together, and I'll be on the way."

He hung up the phone and got up from the sofa. Mr. Rich made it home and saw his wife, Teresa, sitting on the sofa with a glass of wine in her hand. She was sitting in the dark with a few candles burning next to the chair she was sitting in.

"Hey, baby, why are you sitting here in the dark?" She took a sip from her glass.

"Sit down, and talk to me Harold."

He took off his jacket and hung it on the coat rack by the front door. He walked over and sat down across from her on the love seat.

"What's wrong, baby?" his voice was shaky as he asked nervously.

"That man you had over here the other day wasn't an insurance salesman, was he, Harold?"

He just stared at her before he answered because he knew that he had to think of a quick lie. He didn't like bringing any of his dirt into his home because he didn't want to worry or scare his wife.

"Uhhh...Y-Y-Yeah, baby, he was." His voice cracked, and he stuttered as he tried to keep a straight look on his face and sound as honest as possible.

"You're lying to me, Harold. I know when you're lying because you start blinking a lot, and your fingers get to twitching."

Sure enough, Mr. Rich was having a hard time keep his eyes from blinking, and he looked down at his hands and saw that he was twirling his fingers.

"Baby, why would I lie to you about that? You know I wouldn't dare..."

"STOP IT, HAROLD!" By now, Teresa was fed up. The anger came out as she yelled at him. Her voice echoed through the whole house. So loud she could have woke the neighbors.

"Now, Harold, for as long as we've been married I've never got involved with what you do outside this house. I know about all the other women, I know about your gambling problems, and all the money you've lost, but I've never said anything because I love you. Now, my family and friends all called me crazy because I've stayed with you for so long, and I've overlooked all of your wrong doing. But I didn't care because they don't see you as I do. They don't know you like I do."

She stood up and blew out the candles, and then turned the lights on. Her face was red and eyes full of tears. She tried her best to keep them from falling.

"Now, I just can't sit back and let this slide, Harold, tell me the truth." Mr. Rich was speechless.

"Did you really think that I would believe that man was a salesman, Harold?" He shrugged his shoulders.

"I saw that gun he had, Harold." His mouth dropped.

"Yeah, uh huh. You thought that you had gotten over on me again didn't you? Well, I want to know who he is and what does he want with you. Tell me the truth, or else I'm leaving for good." Mr. Rich took a deep breath.

"Ok, Teresa, listen." She held out her hand before he could get another word out.

"Now, think before you speak, Harold, because if you lie, then all of this is over, and I won't look back. I promise you that."

This was the first time he had ever heard her speak like that. For years, she wouldn't say anything about his life outside of home, so he was caught off guard.

"That man was looking for Clarence, baby, he has some business with Clarence, that's all."

She squinted her eyes at him. She knew there was more to it.

"Ok and…" He wanted to leave it at that, but she wasn't giving in.

"And what, Teresa?"

"Don't play stupid, Harold, what did he want with Clarence, and why did he have to come here to talk to you pointing a gun at you if he was just looking for Clarence?"

Mr. Rich stood up and began to walk to the kitchen.

"Harold, don't you walk off; you come back here and talk to me, damn it." He turned and looked at her and saw the look on her face.

"He wanted to ask questions about the boy, Jason, Teresa, ok? Damn." The look she gave him let him know that he needed to give her more.

"Clarence killed Jason Teresa" Her facial expression changed. She was shocked at his confession.

"Well what the hell does he want with you Harold"

"Well I mean it happened in the parking lot of my bar so I guess he figured I knew something and he seems to have it out for Clarence so that's why" She shook her head in disbelief.

"I don't believe that Harold"

That seemed so out of character. Everybody knew Clarence to be such a nice guy. So to hear Mr. Rich say that was a total shock to her. She ran to the coffee table where her cell phone was and picked it up.

"What are you doing, Teresa, who are you calling?" She didn't answer him.

"Umm, hello, nine-one-one, I need—" Before she could even finish, Mr. Rich snatched the phone from her.

"Umm, hello officer. Yeah, everything is fine, sorry to disturb you guys." Teresa tried to grab the phone from him, but he ran into the kitchen.

"Yes, ma'am, I do know that you guys have a lot of work to do and getting prank calls often happen. My wife was just looking for our, umm, our cat." The dispatcher on the other end explained to Mr. Rich not to call unless it was an actual emergency.

"Yes, ma'am, I understand and it won't happen again, thank you." He hung up the phone.

"What the hell did you call the police for, Teresa?" Mr. Rich was upset, and his wife could hear it in his voice.

"We need to tell the police what's going on, Harold."

"Like hell we do, I've known that boy all his life, damn it. I'm not going to throw him under the bus like that."

She continued to shake her head. The anger she had before she found out what was going on turned into fear.

"How do I know that man won't come back and try and shoot you next time, Harold, huh? What if he comes while you're not here and shoots me in the head?" Mr. Rich took a seat on the love seat.

"Teresa, don't worry. Everything will be ok. He won't be coming back."

"Yeah, well what makes you so sure, and what about Clarence? What if the police find out that you know? Don't you know you can get in trouble too?"

He shrugged his shoulders. As they both sat around wondering what to do next, Clarence finally made it to Ashley's apartment. It only took a couple knocks at the door before she opened up. She had been anticipating him.

"Hey, baby, what's wrong?" Clarence asked as he walked inside.

"Clarence, please sit down. There's so much I need to tell you." Clarence sat on the sofa and Ashley sat next to him. She rubbed her stomach as the kicks from the baby increased.

"Clarence, the police came to talk to me." His smile quickly turned upside down.

"What did they say?"

"Well, they didn't say much, Clarence, they were just asking when was the last time I saw you." Clarence dropped his head.

"And what did you tell them?"

"I told them I hadn't seen you in a couple days."

Clarence continued to look at the floor. Ashley placed her hand under his chin to lift his head up. They both looked each other in the eyes.

"Clarence, I haven't been completely honest with you."

He tried to drop his head again but she didn't let him.

"I told you that the doctors said there's a chance I may have cancer." He didn't respond.

"Well, Clarence, I do." His eyes began to water.

"I have breast cancer, Clarence."

A tear slowly rolled down his cheek.

"But the doctor's say that if I go through Chemo, then I should be able to beat it, Clarence." More tears began to fall.

"Don't worry, Clarence, everything will be just fine." She placed both her hands on his face.

"Remember, you told me to trust in God." He closed his eyes.

"We're just gonna have to keep the faith, Clarence." Clarence didn't know what to say.

"But, Clarence, there's something else I need to tell you." He stared into her eyes.

"This is something that's going to hurt you, but I can't keep this from you any longer."

31

Ashley took her time before she made her confession. She made sure she was cautious with how she broke the news to Clarence because he was hurting from the news of her having cancer.

"Clarence, I want to tell you the real reason John has it out for you." He looked up at her with tears in his eyes.

"What are you talking about, Ashley?" By now, tears began to fall from her eyes.

"Clarence, do love you me? I mean, do you even want to be with me?" He didn't respond.

"I mean, do you ever plan on marrying me; we are having a child."

"Didn't you just say you know why John has it out for me? Why are you beating around the bush with all this nonsense, tell me what's going on." Ashley was trying her best to remain calm. But by him saying what she asked him was nonsense, she couldn't hold back.

"You see, Clarence, that's the problem you're so selfish all you care about is yourself. I'm the one carrying this child, and I'm the one who isn't probably going to live much longer, and all you can think about is yourself."

Clarence was confused. How did she go from telling him that she had to break news to him to screaming at him and calling him selfish.

"Ashley, what the hell are you talking about? Don't try and flip this into something else, now you told me that you had something to tell me about John, so what is it? Stop trying to play the victim because I didn't do anything to you."

"Oh you didn't do anything to me, Clarence, are you really going to sit here and say that to my face?" Clarence figured it was the baby that was making her talk the way she was.

"Listen, Ashley. I'm guessing your hormones are doing the talking right now, but I'm not about to sit here and allow you to do this to me."

"Clarence, how many times did you up and leave me by myself? You know how many times I had to go to the doctor by myself? Do you know how many nights I sat by the phone and waited for you to call me? You don't love me, you only love yourself. You're just pretending just because I told you that I was pregnant. I guess you figured you had to do the right thing and stick around; well I don't need you to just stick around. I can do this all by myself since you don't plan on marrying me."

Clarence was speechless. The whole mood had changed. He felt like he was the one who came over to confess doing something wrong. That's the way she made him feel.

"Ashley, I never said that I didn't love you, but how do you expect me to just up and marry after all the stuff you put me through?" She held out her hand and cut him off.

"Stuff I put you through? Are you joking, Clarence, what did I put you through?" All he could do was shake his head.

"Ashley, my best friend who is now dead said that he slept with you and the child that you're carrying is his, and your ex who just so happen to randomly come back into the picture is trying to set me up and get me put in jail. That's what the hell I mean when I say all the stuff you put me through. Stop acting like you're so innocent."

The tension in the room had grown. Both of them were furious.

"Clarence, you know damn well I didn't do anything with Jason, and what about you, huh? How do I know you didn't kill him because you were pretty damn upset when you found out that he said that? How do I know you didn't kill or have him killed, you're such a good liar. I don't know what to believe." Clarence dropped his head.

"You too, Ashley?" Ashley's hormones were raging. She had become so upset basically out of nowhere.

"I really can't believe you would even say that to me, Ashley. I can't believe you would even think that, so since you're talking crazy, I'm just going to leave." He headed for the door but was cut off by Ashley.

"You're not going to leave me alone again, Clarence at least not until I tell you what I have to tell you." He took a few steps back and waited for her to speak.

"John has it out for you because me and him slept together, Clarence." Her confession didn't really get the reaction she expected out of Clarence.

"Ok and…" he shrugged his shoulders and tried to move past her to get to the door.

"What do you mean ok and?"

"Ashley, he's your ex-boyfriend. I'm pretty sure the two of you had sex before, so what, big deal." Ashley closed her eyes and took a deep breath.

"Clarence, that's not what I'm talking about." Clarence reached in his pocket and pulled out his cell phone to check the time.

"Well, what exactly are you talking about, Ashley?" Her heart was so heavy there was no way she could continue to keep it from him anymore.

"Clarence, one night you and me were leaving Mr. Richs bar, and John was coming in, do you remember?" He put his hands into his pockets and nodded his head.

"No, I don't remember."

"Ok, well, anyways, he spoke to me, but I didn't speak back. Well, somehow, he got my number, and he called me a few days later."

"Who the hell did he get your number from?" Clarence's heart was beating very fast. He was anticipating bad news.

"I don't know, Clarence, he never told me." He felt like she was lying or holding something back, but he let her continue

"At first, it started off with us just catching up, and he was telling me about his wife and how she was pregnant. I just assumed he just wanted to keep it on a friendly level."

Clarence pulled his hands out of his pockets. Ashley looked down at his hands as he began to ball them into a fist.

"Well, one night he came over and asked if we could talk."

She made sure she kept a close eye on his hands. She wasn't sure if he were planning on hitting her but he had a look in his eyes that she had never seen before.

"He told me that him and his wife were having problems, and it was around a point in time when you and me weren't getting along, so we both were venting to each other one thing led to another and..."

She stopped. Neither one of them spoke. They just looked each other up and down. Her emotions were all over the place.

"Clarence, I'm so sorry. I never meant for anything to happen, but I was vulnerable and weak." He put his hands back into his pockets.

"Ashley, you just made this big fuss about me not caring about you and not loving you, and then you tell me this."

She tried to respond, but he cut her off before she could utter a word.

"And this man is on my ass saying that I killed Jason, and you've been keeping this from me all this time I was thinking he was just a pure fuckin asshole. Oh, but no, he wants to get back with you. Oh wait, I'm sorry, he already did." More tears began to fall down her face.

"And those tears don't mean a damn thing to me, Ashley, cry me a river, build a bridge, and get over it."

He tried to move past her again, but she wouldn't let him, so he pushed her out the way. Before he reached the door, he turned and said a few more words to her.

"So, let me ask you Ashley is that baby even mine?" Again before she could respond, he cut her off.

"You know what, don't even answer that, I don't even want to hear another one of your lies."

He reached into his pocket and pulled out a box. He opened the box, and inside, there was a big diamond ring.

261

"See, I came over here with intentions of asking you to marry me. Thank God, I didn't make that mistake." He opened the door and walked outside. "Goodbye, Ashley."

32

A couple months went by with Clarence and Ashley both keeping their distance from each other. Ashley was in and out of the doctor. Not just for the baby but also for her cancer. The cancer seemed to be under control since they caught it early, but it did keep her fatigued. Not just the cancer, but the baby as well. She somehow managed to plan a baby shower all by herself. Well, also with limited help from Brittany.

"Well, today is the day, ma'am, are you ready for people to load you up with lots of gifts the baby won't be able to use until he's about five years old?" Ashley looked at her and shook her head.

"Brittany, can you be a little more supportive. I mean, it's bad enough Clarence isn't coming."

She decided to have the shower at her apartment because she didn't have the energy to do it anywhere else. As she picked up a box and tried to move it to the kitchen, she dropped the box after taking a couple steps. She grabbed her stomach and began to scream. Brittany ran to her and grabbed her just as she began to fall to the floor.

"ASHLEY, WHAT'S WRONG?" Brittany yelled out frantically.

"Brittany, I think this baby is trying to come early."

She still had about a month to go, so it came to a surprise to Brittany.

"What do you mean it's trying to come? I'm not ready." Ashley glared at her. "I mean, you're not ready."

Ashley was breathing fast. The contractions were coming closer and closer. She walked to the kitchen counter and grabbed her purse and keys.

"Look, Brittany, if you don't want to take me to the hospital so I can have this baby, I'll drive my damn self."

She pulled her cell phone out of her purse and called Clarence, but he didn't answer. She almost threw the phone to the ground, but she sent him a text message letting him know that the baby was coming.

"Like hell you will."

Brittany snatched her keys from her.

"I'm going to drive you, and we're going to go have this baby."

She rushed to the front door, and they both made their way out. Brittany sped to the hospital. The whole ride there was very hectic as Ashley was in the backseat screaming her lungs out. It got to a point to where Brittany thought she'd have to pull the car over so they could deliver the baby on the side of the road. Once they made it to the hospital, Brittany pulled up right in front of the emergency entrance. She jumped out of the car and ran to the back door to let Ashley out. One of the employees who was outside having as smoke break ran up to them before they made it into the hospital.

"Ma'am, you can't park right there. It's a hazard."

Brittany tossed him the car keys.

"Well, sir you park the car. Can't you see we're trying to deliver this baby?"

She and Ashley made their way into the hospital. They walked up to the front desk and were greeted by a doctor who was speaking to a woman in the clerical area.

"Doctor, she's getting ready to have this baby."

The doctor hurried up and turned his attention to them. He ran across the lobby and grabbed a wheelchair and pushed it over to Ashley and told her to sit down. She sat in the wheelchair and he pushed her through the double doors and Brittany followed behind.

"What's your doctor's name, ma'am?"

Ashley was in so much pain she couldn't respond. She was screaming from the contractions. He turned and asked Brittany as they raced to an empty room. Brittany shrugged her shoulders. They finally found a room, and the doctor was able to help Ashley get into the bed. He left the room for a couple minutes as he tried to find her doctor. Doctors scrambled into the room. All ready to deliver her baby. They allowed Brittany to stay in the room as all the action went on. After all the commotion, there was the sound of a baby crying, and Brittany uncovered her eyes to see the doctor handing the new born to Ashley. Brittany began to cry. Most of the doctors clapped and said congratulations and then left the room.

"Where's, Clarence?" Ashley's doctor asked as she stared at her baby boy.

"Umm, he was stuck in traffic the last time we spoke with him, and he should be arriving any minute now."

Brittany answered the doctor's question before Ashley had a chance to respond. The doctor looked on as if he knew there was more than traffic keeping Clarence from being there to witness the birth of the baby. He watched as Ashley held the baby, and Brittany leaned over the bed asking to hold him. Ashley was hesitant at first, as first time mothers usually are when someone asks to hold their child. She eventually gave in. A few minutes later, surprisingly, Clarence walked into the room. Brittany's mouth dropped. It was very unexpected. She thought she'd never see him again. Not because of the issues between him and Ashley but for other reasons. Brittany walked over to him and handed him the baby. She then walked over to Ashley and gave her a kiss on the forehead.

"I'll leave you guy's be. I'll be back later."

The doctor followed behind her. The two of them didn't speak much just a few words. Clarence didn't stay long either, he told her he had to get back to work. The doctors came back in and took the baby to the newborn delivery room. Ashley called Clarence to ask him why he didn't stay, but he didn't answer the phone. She wasn't as upset with him as she was with herself. She questioned whether or not she should have told him what happened between her and John. It seemed to have ruined everything between her and Clarence. It tore them apart at the worst possible time.

33

Ashley was able to go home with the baby after a couple days. She was able to get settled in with her newborn and began getting accustomed to being a first time mother. Clarence called her a few times to check on her and the baby, but he didn't come by to check on them. She had help from Brittany. Who seemed to be more excited about the baby more than everyone. A few months had passed by and still no sign of Clarence. Everyone's lives began to change. Ashley was trying to get used to being a single mother, and the cancer in her breasts began to spread so she was really getting sick as time went on. Most days, she stayed in the bed, and Brittany had to care for the child as Ashley would sleep. She even began to lose her hair. She and Clarence would talk every day, but he still wouldn't come around. Clarence was still having issues of his own as he was being harassed by the police. They were still trying to piece things together and find Jason's killer. John was making it his business to try and make Clarence's life a living hell. Which he was actually successful at. Clarence would barely leave the house unless it was for work. Mr. Rich even found himself trying to be low key as well. He had a few run INS with John when he would show up at the bar. John was putting pressure on everyone. At times, he even tried to contact Ashley, but he failed because she eventually changed her number. Ashley's cancer had begun to get serious, and it forced her into the hospital. She lost all of her hair, and most nights she stayed up crying. At one point in time, she felt like she was on top of the world. She had a man, who loved her, and they were having a child but after many mishaps, things just took a turn for the worst, and she felt like life hit her the hardest.

One day, she sat in the hospital bed and stared at the wall. Her doctor came in to check on her and asked her how she was feeling, but she wouldn't even respond. He told her that he knew something that would make her smile. She didn't really pay any attention to him because she felt as if her life was pretty much over. He left the room and five minutes later there was a knock at the door. Ashley didn't even react. In walked Clarence. Ashley didn't even turn to see who it was coming into the room. He walked up to the side of the bed and called out to her.

"Hello my, sweetheart." Ashley turned slowly as she recognized his voice. Her mouth dropped as she saw Clarence had shaved his head bald to match hers. He was wearing an all-black tuxedo with a pink tie.

"Clarence, what are you doing here, and why are you wearing that suit?"

"Ashley, I know that things haven't gone the way we expected, and life has thrown many obstacles our way, and I apologize for everything that I've put you through. I feel as if I have not been by your side the way I should have been. I have done a horrible job, and I know that I've broken your heart more than once."

Tears began to roll down his face. Usually, Ashley was the first to cry but this time it was Clarence. Not long after though, she began to cry as well.

"I was hoping to come in here and make amends, I know that is not the easiest thing to do, but I figured I'd come in and try."

He dropped to one knee and reached into his pocket then pulled out that same diamond ring that he had shown her before. She began to cry even more.

"Ashley. I want to spend the rest of my life with you and as soon as we get you out of this hospital, we're going to get a new place and be a happy family. I want you to be my wife not just the mother of my child."

Ashley could barely control herself.

"Yes, Clarence, I will marry you."

Her smile was so big and the tears continued to fall. In walked a reverend holding a bible in his hand. The nurses were dressed up as bridesmaids and her doctor was the best man. She was so surprised. Clarence had planned the whole thing out with the help of her best friend Brittany. Brittany walked in holding their son. Of course she accepted the role of the maid of honor. The reverend performed an actual ceremony and they were married right there in the hospital. Just when Ashley felt like her life had hit rock bottom Clarence came in and saved the day completely.

Afterwards, he told her that he was going to go and change his clothes to get more comfortable. She asked him to go and get her some food from outside of the hospital because she had grown tired of eating the same thing. The burger joint he went to took a little longer than expected but he was finally able to place his order and he raced back to the hospital to be with his new wife. Just as he walked towards her room, the doctor walked out shaking his head and had a very concerned look on his face. He tried to stop Clarence, but Clarence feared the worst as he looked the doctor in his eyes. He dropped the food to the ground and pushed the doctor out of the way. As he bust through the door he saw Brittany on her knees crying. One of the nurses had taken their baby boy out of the room. Ashley laid with her eyes closed. Clarence never got the chance to say goodbye. It was too late, Ashley was gone. Clarence stayed on the floor as long as the doctors allowed him. One of the doctor's came in and told him that he was going to have to leave the room. As he was walking out, John and two officers approached him.

"Hello, Clarence good to see you again, sir."

He spoke with a huge grin on his face. Clarence didn't budge.

"I'm sorry to inform you that you're under arrest for murder."

Clarence didn't even try to fight or resist. He even put his hands behind his back and the officers put the cuffs on his wrists and took him out of the hospital.

Made in the USA
Charleston, SC
22 July 2014